BIG
THINKING
FOR SMALL BUSINESS

STRAIGHTFORWARD ADVICE
TO GROW YOUR BUSINESS

STEVEN J COULSON

GW00569768

RETHINK PRESS

First published in Great Britain in 2020
by Rethink Press (www.rethinkpress.com)

Contents

Introduction

Looking back to when I first started running my own business in 2000, the one thing I now wish I had was a mentor. Someone who'd sit down, spend some time with me and dish out some straight-talking, no-nonsense advice. Someone who had started out in business, just like I was about to, and could tell me, 'This is what we found, this is what happened to us, these are the pitfalls, this is what you might want to look out for.' It could be anything from how to avoid common mistakes, to knowing how to recruit the right people, understanding the accounting basics, managing operations, marketing and sales and, ultimately, how to scale up without the need for expensive venture capital or private equity. I wasn't trying to be the next Bill Gates, I just wanted to be in control of my life and to feel like I was winning.

When I took my first solo steps, I was blind as blind can be and I simply hoped for the best. After all, I was following my dream to somehow, someday, run a successful business that I could be proud of and also make a decent living from.

Today, I can hold my head up high and say I've achieved that aim, but I learned it the hard way and I've taken my fair share of knocks in the process. If I'd had a mentor at the start, I would've had a better idea of how to avoid some of the obstacles I've encountered. Of course, there's a mountain of excellent self-help books available that cover every conceivable aspect of business know-how but, in my opinion, that's also part of the problem. What if you're simply stuck and want to find a way of growing your business, be that making brass tacks, some high-tech gadget or simply expanding your local fish-and-chip shop? Growing and scaling up your business doesn't need to be the next unicorn idea, although plenty of books show you how you can change the world if you have that one earth-shattering vision. What if you're not the next Uber, Airbnb, eBay, ASOS or Richard Branson in the making? Instead, you're a down-to-earth business owner or start-up with a solid product or service, yours is an SME (small- to medium-sized enterprise) with a handful of employees, and the time is right to go to the next stage. Except you're not looking for investors to take your shares and control away, you don't want to study for a business degree, and you really don't want to plough your way through the plethora of well-intentioned books (after all, you have a business to run). Don't get me wrong, much of that content is amazing, but there's probably only half a chapter in each that will benefit you, while the remainder may be too advanced/specialist in relation to business maturity, or simply irrelevant to your needs. For my part, I've always learned most when I've listened to others who have been on the journey ahead of me and heard what their experiences have been.

This is the primary reason why I wanted to write this book. I wanted to share my practical experience of building a business from scratch, growing it, selling it, building another, scaling it, and now continuing to thrive. I'm not offering you highbrow theoretical solutions – this is a practical, warts-and-all book based on my own learning. What you'll get is a no-bullshit guide where I can share the pitfalls, what the real wins are and all the things you didn't know you needed to look out for. It doesn't matter that your business looks nothing like my own – the principles are the same for any micro-business or SME. Therefore, if you're feeling stuck and need some solid, reliable, practical guidance that works, you're in good hands. Even though I can't physically be in the same room as you, I'd like you to regard this book as your first mentor. Just like the one I wish I had had all those years back.

If I'm honest, at that time the odds were stacked against me. I didn't like school or do particularly well there, and I've since learned, after my son was diagnosed with attention deficit hyperactivity disorder (ADHD), that I also suffered from this condition as a kid. I left school at fifteen and went to sea to work on the Arctic trawlers, right up into the North Cape of Norway, Bear Island and Spitsbergen. Those were long, tough days (and nights) but I learned how to work, and what work meant. I must have gained a liking for the sea because I then joined the Royal Navy for five years and travelled the world. While on deployment in the South Atlantic I first saw the film *Wall Street* on our Saturday night 'film night' event. For whatever reason, something inside me clicked and the film resonated deep within me. I realised that I wanted to be in business (probably not with Gordon Gekko's business ethics, thankfully) and while still on board ship, I began studying for a Higher National Diploma (HND) in business and finance by distance learning. I did my private study after coming off a twelve-hour watch and sat at a table with the ship rolling this way and that, trying to understand marketing, balance sheets and contract law. Back on dry land I passed the HND, left the Navy and worked my way through dead-end admin jobs until I met my future business partners in a small firm in Wakefield.

Today, I'm happy to say we own our second business, where we enable organisations to realise the huge opportunities that commercial drones bring to their operations. We learned business the hard way, without any mentors or fancy words in fancy business books.

Yet this business grew 140% within a twelve-month period and continues to grow apace to the extent that I'm confident we'll make the Fast Track 100 next year (as we did with our previous business, so the pressure's on). We ran our first business for eighteen years and it was sold to a PLC in January 2019 for an eight-figure sum. We achieved all this from humble beginnings in a way that didn't involve any private equity or venture capital (brilliant routes to follow for many emerging businesses, but that's not our experience), and our growth path could just as well apply to your business too. Just like you, we had dreams of success, of being able to build businesses that we could eventually scale up from a couple of employees to something more substantial, possibly with ambitions to enter the international marketplace. The nature of such ambitions doesn't matter here; it's following a vision and attaining the success you want to achieve that matters. It's knowing how to overcome the barriers that keep getting in your way, be they financial, institutional, psychological and, dare I say, emotional. I'd wager that many small business owners not born with a silver spoon in their mouths or never expecting to be the next Elon Musk harbour a variety of self-limiting beliefs that keep them stuck where they are. Believe me, there's nothing wrong with being 'ordinary'. I'm rightly proud of my roots in Wakefield and no matter what I might believe in, one thing I do know has served me well is my willingness to put in some hard graft, no matter what the task in hand might be. Just like you do with your own business right now. You still have dreams and aspirations for the future, you still want to leave some kind of legacy, and even though your business might not be the next world-dominating unicorn, that should not hold you back. So, what if yours is a fish-and-chip shop by the seaside? Knowing how to go for it can make all the difference, and yours could be the best in town, on the coast, or even in the country for that matter. There's still a small fortune to be made and doing so will give you a huge sense of personal satisfaction. It's not just about the money: it's also about following your vision.

Too often, one of the biggest barriers to our success is having that kind of dream but believing we need to redefine ourselves as a result. And yet, you don't have to redefine yourself by anyone else's standards in the hope your business will become the Uber of fish-and-chip shops, or of springs or bolts. Of course, radical disruptors such as Uber have played a huge part in shaping how businesses run and operate. You could be forgiven for thinking that your business can't compete with the likes of these giants. I disagree. In terms of your own impact, it's amazingly possible to disrupt in so many different ways across any industry, no matter the size and ambition of the business. When it's been done a million times before, simply taking a slightly different approach can set one business apart from the rest. You might think, 'That's not disrupting', but if you grew a reputation for providing the best customer service *ever* in your sector, it would blow your customers (and competition) away. As a result, your reputation would continue to grow and – hey presto – you've become the disruptor who's known the length and the breadth of the country.

Much of that will be down to you. Don't forget, your individuality is actually one of your biggest *assets*; always be humble enough to learn and never lose your drive and vision. Do what you want to do, because if you read every business book, take every form of advice and spend hours listening to every podcast, you can quickly lose direction, followed by confidence, and end up believing you're doing everything wrong. It's no bad thing to hold onto the fact that you *don't* know everything and *can't* be everything to everybody. It's true what they say: 'Serve everybody, and you serve nobody.' There's no sentiment from the market.

My aim, therefore, is that by the time you finish reading this book you'll have regained confidence in yourself, your vision and your business. I'll share my experiences candidly, including the ups and downs and everything that I've learned (and by the way, I'm *still* learning) about setting up a business, finding the right people to work with, dealing with the money, reaching out to customers and converting leads into sales. I'll only ever be straight with you and I won't beat about the bush. I won't shy away from the hard facts, because I believe that honesty is a liberator.

By the end of this book, you should be able to hold true to all the brilliant qualities you have and at the same time face any business situation with brutal honesty. That way you'll be able to do something about it. It's as good a place as any to begin building the business of your dreams.

1
Honest Self-appraisal

Either you're an industrious, hardworking small business owner, or you're someone who's looking to establish a new business now, or in the near future. Whichever category you fall into, the common denominator is that you have a vision of how it will develop and an ambition to scale it up so that it provides for you and your family. For whatever reason, however, you feel like you've been 'on hold' and now you've been compelled to make a change in your life. Something has triggered your desire for more; you might feel you're stuck in a rut in your business, job, or perhaps been made redundant which has given you a sum of money. No matter how you've reached this point, you're passionate about your future business vision. You might be lucky enough to have some funding in place, but even if not, you're excited at the prospect of what lies ahead in the next six to twelve months.

However, you're aware that excitement and passion alone are not enough. You know potential roadblocks and hurdles lie ahead and you're unsure how to navigate them. These may be your own doubts and uncertainties leading to your current indecision, to the extent you're not sure if you're doing the right thing at all. As a result, you feel blocked, not knowing which way to turn or whose opinion to trust the most. Family and friends all want the best for you, but their thoughts and advice might not be appropriate, or what you want to hear. You feel lost and hemmed in by these walls of doubt, especially if your business is up and running but you can't afford to pay yourself, even though you ensure that you pay your employees first while suppliers bang on your door. The vision you once had now seems lost in a fog, or it seems so unattainable you no longer know how to achieve it. The result is, you feel like you've come full circle and that you're stuck like a hamster on its wheel. Various business self-help books have only filled you with scant confidence, as you read about other (especially unicorn) businesses achieving X, Y and Z success. You, however, remain stuck at A, B and C.

The problem is, you're comparing yourself to potentially unrelated, and unfair, examples against which you measure your own shortcomings. It's a self-fulfilling prophecy – you're never going to make it or find the funds to kick-start your own dream. It's never occurred to you that many of those successful businesses might never have done it under their own steam as you're attempting to do. The effect of this conflicting, hyper-inflated information is that you're now *overthinking* your proposition, without considering your own circumstances. The danger is, you'll end up diluting it in a knee-jerk response to your fears and self-doubts.

It's time we sat down and talked.

Brutal facts

My first piece of advice is, don't give up. Whether you're starting out, or you've reached a crisis point, or you simply want to know how to grow your business, giving up is the easy option when you feel lost, unsupported or conflicted. When you're faced with so many barriers, pursuing your dreams under these conditions can feel daunting, as I know only too well. What's needed is a healthy dose of brutally honest self-reflection.

Firstly, take a step back, even if that feels counterintuitive. Your instinct tells you to spend hours on the shop floor, because you feel the need to be busy (but this is 'busy fool' syndrome). Resist that and get away from your normal humdrum existence, remove yourself from all distractions, no matter how hard that feels. You'll be needing both space and time to ask yourself some brutally honest questions that require equally honest answers. You can't do this in front of your computer, or from the comfort of your own home – you need to escape all distractions. That might initially come as a shock to those nearest to you, so communicate this clearly with your loved ones, family and friends. Tell them it's necessary time for you, because any sudden, out-of-character 'disappearance' can be unsettling and only increases pressure on them, and you. Even if they don't immediately fully understand your reasons, proactively communicating your intent is key. Knowing that you have their respect for telling them is one thing less for you to worry about.

Choose somewhere you can go and clear your head in preparation for the questions you need to ask yourself. Get away for the weekend, stay in a cabin or rent a small cottage. This is about making way for clear and conscious focus. When you find that space, you'll have the time and energy to ask yourself the questions about your business that you've been long putting off:

• What's the current state of the business?

• Is my business plan up to scratch?

• Is it a viable business?

- Will it ultimately deliver a six-figure salary, year on year?

- Will it grow and sustain other people's livelihoods?

- Will it live up to my vision?

- Do I have the heart and passion for the testing journey ahead?

- Is it a real business, or is it a hobby?

- Or is it just a pipe dream?

These are undoubtedly difficult, searching questions because they raise your head above the honesty parapet. However, they also remind you about what first ignited your passion and fed your initial excitement. In making time to reflect on your original business vision, if you can honestly say that you're still hungry and passionate, that's the reason why you'll jump out of bed each morning to make it a reality.

Honest answers

Having responded with brutal honesty and still hungry for success, can you truthfully say that you're offering products or services that your customers really want? If they're not buying from you, then, in its current set-up, yours might not be a viable business. It's not the end of the road:

- Invite and analyse feedback from your customers and, if needed, implement any changes to your offering.

- Give your business the best opportunities it can have to shine and grow in your market sector and/or locale.

- Raise the bar so that your business stands out but set realistic, achievable goals.

It doesn't need to be the best within the next six or twelve months, or even within the next three years, but eventually its aim will to be the best. Think big and think ahead to the point where you're capable and equipped to scale up your business, as opposed to running a small business in a small town and standing still. Aiming to be the best at what you do in your county, region or even the world tells you that you have a growth mind-set.

Meanwhile, can the business pay you? Too often, business owners sacrifice their own salary in order to pay others or to honour financial commitments. The business might be breaking even, or making a small profit, but you're still the one taking the risks. On that basis, determine whether the business can pay you a viable salary within a realistic timeframe (dependent on your own circumstances). If it can't, then consider changing what your business is, or revising your business plan. Otherwise it's just a hobby and a potentially expensive one at that. Brutal, I know.

A growth mind-set

Never underestimate the value of gaining more knowledge and skills – this is an essential element for future success. There's complete truth behind the adage, 'You can't earn more than you learn'. If you don't currently have a personal mentor to advise you, there are still numerous ways you can expand your knowledge and skills. Often, I hear people say they don't have enough time to plough through the plethora of online digital resources, such as podcasts and audiobooks, or even to read real books. I dispute that: there's always time. If that means going to bed an hour earlier in order to get up an hour earlier before the business day begins, then so be it. The truth is, we all have plenty of spare time just walking around, so my advice (and my own practice) is to turn that time into something useful. You need to own the day with an early start and make sure you fill the whole time with full value to you – and I do include good sleep in that equation. The brutal fact is that most of us waste most of our time in our days with things that don't help us grow as people. This is fatal for a business owner who's wanting to grow.

Personally, I consume a wide variety of educational and informational podcasts from when I get out of bed at 5:00am until I arrive at 7:30am, and the same on the way home. As a result, I achieve an extra four to five hours personal growth each day without doing anything differently. That equates to at least twenty hours per week learning. Those marginal gains add up and the results flow into my days, my plans and my leadership. I've discovered that by changing how my day is structured (early to bed, early to rise) I achieve much more. I try to focus on income-generating tasks during regular business hours, and deal with emails later in the day when there are less distractions. I've also learned to be more patient and reflective, and not to make decisions based on emotion. Learning something seemingly small, such as saying 'please' and 'thank you' more often, also keeps the ego in check and I then find that people I work with are more responsive, giving and productive. That helps makes any business more successful.

Growth, through learning, is one of my top tips for helping you to grow your business. For me, it's an essential tool. The fact is, your business or your vision won't grow if your mind-set is also not about growth.

I now realise I had the start of a growth mind-set as far back as 1989. I had just returned to UK shores following an eight-month deployment to Brazil. During that time, I'd been constantly thinking about what exactly I wanted to do with my life. I knew my future didn't lie long term in the Royal Navy, or at sea. For some reason, after I'd seen *Wall Street* on board ship, its theme resonated with me, and it triggered my entrepreneurial gene. When I eventually returned home, I became curious and then obsessed about people's shopping habits and asked myself, 'Why do we spend so much time driving to the supermarket? There must be a way to bring the supermarket to people.' At that time, I was a junior rating and not exactly earning a huge wage and so I had little money to fritter away in the bars in Southsea. Instead, I invested in a notepad and took to wandering around supermarkets noting how much stock they carried in dry goods, and fresh and frozen foods. Inside my head, the germ of an idea was growing – I was mapping it all out because I wanted to replicate what the supermarkets provided by offering a home delivery service where customers would phone in their orders. Bear in mind this all pre-dates the onset of internet shopping as we now know it, but at least my instincts were proved right. I didn't have the experience, knowledge or resources to take the idea forward, but my entrepreneurial juices were flowing. In theory, I was a 'disruptor', even though I didn't yet know the significance of that.

It was as if a safety seal in my mind had been broken. I'd been brought up in a tight and disciplined environment. When I left school I immediately went to sea. Hence, I'd always found myself governed by the strictest of rules. Watching *Wall Street*, then teaching myself about the retail world, prompted me to ask, 'Why do I need to follow what everybody else does?' That innate connection to my sense of individuality is one of the reasons I'm in business today and it's that same mind-set that's always helped me through periods when I've felt stuck. I know that deep down, I'm a disruptor who wants to make a change, and a difference, in the marketplace. That early desire to disrupt, as I now know it, stemmed from having a growth mind-set developed through learning.

Knowing your market

Knowing your market is essential, and being connected to your sense of individuality, combined with a capacity for learning, is key to your future growth. When you feel stuck, or unsure about how to go to the next level, take a look at the following questions and be brutally honest with your answers:

- Where are you in the market and how does your offer compare to the competition?

- Who are your competitors and what are their strengths and weaknesses?

- What market share do you really have?

It's not good enough simply to say, 'I don't know' because with a little effort on your part, you'll soon gain insights to each of the above through carrying out research. It's time well spent in understanding where your business sits. Even if you discover that your market share is 0.01% you then know you've got 99.99% of the market as a possibility. If, on the other hand, you are completely stagnant and not making any money at all, then it's time either to try and change the market, or to get out of that market completely. Knowing the competitive landscape and how much of a share you occupy will answer your questions, one way or another. Therefore, learn and discover as much as you can about your competition.

It's not such a labour-intensive exercise as it was for me back in 1989, because there are so many new tools available at your fingertips. Obviously, internet search engines and Companies House records are immediately accessible and fantastic resources to begin with. However, there's nothing as good as simply picking up the phone, posing as a potential customer and listening to your competitors' sales processes, or even visiting their premises, especially if you're involved in retail. Seeing your competition in action first-hand can provide you with useful information, but ensure you return on different days and at different times to observe customer footfall variations and look at what they're buying. If your business happens to be fish and chips and your premises has only three customers on a Tuesday night, while two streets down they're queuing out of the door, you'll soon learn what the competition's unique selling points are. Don't be disheartened by what you discover; instead, view this as an opportunity to learn and grow your own market share. Ask the people in your competitor's queue why they think this is the best chip shop in the area. It might be nothing more significant than its location, on an estate or outside a factory, and little to do with the quality of the fish and chips. Collate all the information in a matrix or a spreadsheet that you can revisit and update. We've used a competitor matrix on many occasions to position ourselves outside the reach of our competition.

Your customers are also part of your knowledge bank, so ignore them at your peril. I'm still surprised to discover business owners who don't look for customer feedback. Their input is essential to your growth, as it's through them you'll discover where you need to add more value or improve your offering. It might result in having to invest more in producing/distributing your products in return for a lower margin, but if your volume turnover increases, your profit will too, and this will enable you to scale up. The hard truth is that what prevents some businesses from growing might just be the fear of *actually growing* and what will happen if they grow too quickly, taking them into uncharted territory. They're scared that something's bound to go wrong.

[WIIFM + FMOB + SFW] = differentiation

No, I've not printed a line from an algebra textbook by mistake. Instead, it's a prompt point to ask yourself, what's your unique value to the customer? If you don't already know, look at the question from your customers' perspective: 'What's in it for me?' (or WIIFM, as I call it). Translated, that means: are you providing unique value? This leads to another key question, 'What persuades your customer to purchase from you? Are you FMOB?'

- First

- Most

- Only

- Best

The FMOB test helps you identify what differentiates your points of unique value. Now run your findings through the SFW indicator (So f*****g what?). It's a surprisingly useful test that I often use, and you're probably wondering how to apply it. Let me explain using my fish-and-chip shop example. If yours is the only unit that serves its chips in blue polystyrene boxes, that might not pass the SFW test. If, on the other hand, you only fry using a certain oil that's tasty, but is also healthier, that would pass the SFW test because it differentiates you from the competition, attracts custom and provides unique value.

I often wonder what would have happened if brands, such as Kodak or BlackBerry, had put themselves through the [WIIFM + FMOB + SFW] test. Kodak, for example, never seemed to grasp the brutal fact that digital imaging was emerging as a dominant market share, despite the fact they'd actually invented it. If Kodak's executive team had taken itself away for a weekend, as I described at the beginning of the chapter, and been ruthlessly honest about their product and changing consumer trends, the brand might have long survived and dominated. The fact they owned the intellectual property (IP) in the technology meant they could have uniquely differentiated themselves from the competition and gained market dominance. Similarly, the leaders at RIM Technology (owners of BlackBerry) lost sight of their mainly corporate customer base preference for their products. In attempting to compete with Apple's sexier, shinier iPhone (more geared towards consumer tastes) they seemed to abandon all that was unique about their product. That strategic decision, or the lack of applying the [WIIFM + FMOB + SFW] test, killed them.

If I can do it, so can you

I've learned from experience that asking myself difficult questions is both valuable and productive. When the infamous credit crunch of 2008 hit, many business owners, myself included, were forced to ask some deep and searching questions. I took myself to a country hotel on the Northumberland coast and spent the weekend walking the beaches, going over and over those brutal questions, while trying to work my way through the answers. At the time, the business was highly profitable and growing fast (we'd been in the UK Fast Track 100 a couple years earlier) with just under £6m turnover per annum, and with a future order book equivalent to roughly the same amount. Much of the business relied on orders from shipyards based in the Far East, but within the space of a week those orders had been cancelled, leaving us with just under half the £6m we were expecting. Within a month, those orders were barely worth £500k. All incoming emails slowed to a trickle and the phones stopped ringing almost overnight because the whole industry, based on the finance sector supporting the building and purchase of ships, had been severely impacted by the global economic crisis.

Only by facing brutal facts head on could we find the solutions to our problems. There were no easy answers, and we knew some hard decisions were being forced upon us. We needed to act quickly. Immediately, we suspended all directors' salaries and, unfortunately, we laid off 20% of our workforce. We also placed the whole business on a four-day week, to be reviewed in three months. Fact-facing and acting decisively on the outcomes, we avoided those 'salami cuts' that saw other businesses slowly disappear. Because we faced the brutal facts with honesty and without ego, we acted decisively and managed to save the business. Within three months, we'd returned to a five-day week.

2

Understanding Your Growth Mind-set and What Makes You Tick

As a young man, before I started out in business, I now know I didn't have a full growth mind-set. I was a 'rebel', a self-styled 'cock o' the North' ready to take on the world, and everyone in it. In truth, I didn't have a clue about what was needed in business, although I had plenty of energy. Looking back, I realise much of that was *negative* energy; everywhere I turned, I only saw obstacles with a 'that won't work' response, and I was blind to opportunities. My natural default was to judge everyone, and everything, and I wasn't at all curious about how others achieved success. I certainly didn't celebrate other people's success and I didn't appreciate excellence. I simply thought people were luckier than me. That pretty much sums me up as a young man, a negative thinker with a short-term mind-set. I think I was typical of many young British adults who were raised as kids in the 1970s and 1980s. Whereas, across the pond, when Bruce Springsteen sang 'Born in the U.S.A.', American kids knew immediately what that meant and could picture the all-American dream. More to the point, it was *their* American dream. 'Rule Britannia' didn't quite have the same ring about it. The US has always embraced a culture of personal growth and so its people naturally viewed (and still view) success as something to celebrate, emulate and replicate.

It wasn't until the late 1990s that I suddenly realised I'd been spending (and wasting) a huge amount of exhausting, negative energy, thanks to my closed mind-set. It dawned on me that the person standing in the way of my success was *me*. Meeting my future business partners was the catalyst for me to develop my growth mind-set. It wasn't an instant conversion, instead it was an iterative, gradual process. Now, I constantly want to know, what can I learn from other people? When once I was a 'jack the lad', these days I'm humbler and I approach the 'unknown' with a sense of wonder, and without negative judgement. Therefore, when I refer to a 'growth mind-set' it's not 'new age' jargon, it's an essential tool for business, equally important as any you might use on the factory floor, in your shop, or in any other business activity.

The learning continuum

As humans, we only truly start to learn when we're open to learning. Children are born with a growth mind-set in how they see the world for the first time and learn to walk and talk. As their brains and thirst for knowledge expand, we send them to school. Although sadly, for so many, learning stops the moment they leave. Nobody can truthfully say anyone is equipped to know everything at that age. Otherwise, why do we often find ourselves stuck in later life? We need to carry on learning.

Experiential learning is all well and good but it can be a slow curve. What might take fifty years to fathom doesn't sound like success to me. On the other hand, being open to learning could shorten that curve from fifty years to five months through listening to podcasts and audiobooks, attending 'masterclasses', finding mentors and reading books. Learning from other people, even if their own business is in no way related to your own, is one of the best ways you'll be able to translate and apply their experience to your own. It's one of the primary reasons I was motivated to write this book, after all. And the more I learn, the more I want to know. Embracing your own growth mind-set creates an abundance of ideas, plans and opportunities to scale up. Continual learning is your route to making your business better and bigger. It's the key that unlocks your dreams.

The good news is that, unlike school, or being stuck in a regimented job, there are no rules, apart from being open to learning. Think of yourself as an elite athlete; not only do you need to put in the hard graft each day and train, you also need to engage your brain. A significant part of an athlete's training involves sport psychology. Athletes know they need their head to be in the right place before they step onto the track to win gold. If the track is your business journey, your own head also needs to be in the right place if you also want to beat the competition and win gold.

As I mentioned in Chapter 1, avoid the mistake of telling yourself, 'I don't have the time.' If your business manufactures widgets, for example, from 8am to 6pm, that doesn't mean that time is in short supply. If you're really hungry for success, and you want to grow and scale up, start your own day earlier, and use that time to listen to the audiobook autobiography of the person closest to your industry, or anyone else you admire who's been successful in business. I guarantee you'll hear some nugget of inspiration that will resonate with you. It might not solve all your problems, but learning, no matter how you consume it, will help point you in the right direction. At the same time, the exercise releases more endorphins that create a powerful mix of positivity, amplifying the learning. However, if you consider learning to be outside of your comfort zone, then you have two simple choices: give up your business right now, or choose to embrace learning.

I'll assume you'll choose option 2. You have a business to grow. The fact you're stuck and don't know how to scale up is a new discomfort zone. What's the risk in being open to learning? I'm not talking about endless study, taking exams, or adding to your stress. I want you to *enjoy* the learning process. You could do worse than simply talking with, and listening to, businesspeople near you, who just might have brilliant things to say that you don't need a PhD to understand. Or, listen to a podcast from any inspirational speaker and you'll extract what's most useful for you. What's really so discomforting about an audiobook, or reading in private, compared to the brave and bold steps you've already taken in setting up your business? I'll admit I used my own fear of learning to hold me back. Then I realised I needed to confront this self-limitation. For example, in my early days, I was terrified of speaking in public. I'd break out in a cold sweat and rush and stumble over my words, often forgetting the order they needed to be in; quite frankly, I'd make a hash of it. However, I knew speaking in public was an essential skill I needed to learn, and so I persevered. I took a course on the best techniques and over time I grew less afraid of my audience the more confident I became. If anyone had told me in the 1990s that a few years later I'd end up delivering a stand-up comedy gig in front of a crowd of 400 people, I wouldn't have believed them. But after years of persistent learning, I did it. What's more, I loved it and now I relish the chance to speak in public. To be honest, it didn't always feel good at first, but it always felt amazing afterwards.

Learning to let go

Not everyone in your current friendship circle will understand why you're spending less time with them and more on learning. This is one of the hardest elements to learn – to let go. You have two further choices:

1. Be open to learning through listening and reading to help develop your growth mind-set.

2. Or, read the book on how to stay best friends with closed mind-set friends down the pub and remain dissatisfied with your business and personal growth.

Like me, you'll soon discover that not everyone around you will share your interests or ambitions. However, if you end up as the cleverest person in the room, then you need to start meeting people cleverer, or further ahead of you, who share the same interests and ideologies, as that will supercharge your learning. If you surround yourself with people who belittle your vision and your dream, you'll end up achieving nothing. My hope is that, because you're reading this book, intuitively you already know this, but you might not have translated it into conscious action. We all remember the jokers in the classroom disrupting the learning process, who pulling everyone else down, but it's something we just put up with. It was our default, our normalised response. If you haven't already done so, it's time to *un*learn that learned response if you want to grow.

Inevitably, that requires a certain level of sacrifice. Let go of that behaviour and the people around you who perpetuate it. There's no need to be confrontational; instead, embed your learning practice into your everyday life by seeking out others who also want to learn. In time, you'll be the one that other business-people seek out to learn from.

One book that I highly recommend, which had a profound impact on my own learning pathway, is *The Chimp Paradox: The Mind Management Programme to Help You Achieve Success, Confidence and Happiness* by Professor Steven Peters. It was fundamental in improving my intrinsic learning capabilities which then freed up the space I needed to improve my extrinsic capabilities, such as dealing with the practicalities of running a business. Prior to that, my lack of intrinsic skills held me back (including my short temper and low attention span). I became curious as to how human psychology works and where it stems from. Once you grasp the basics of psychology you can manage it and understand more about how our own internal engines work. You'll gain valuable insights into what makes you, other people, and your business tick.

The moment my tick clicked

I grew up in the belief I was hemmed in by a series of rules that went against my grain. However, that was all I knew and, in many ways, it explains how and why I joined the Navy with its regimented structure. After that, I took a series of humdrum jobs but with no real idea of what I really wanted to do. I didn't even know what sparked my interest. All I was certain of was that being employed as a surgical buyer for the NHS, with people chasing me for pacemakers that I hadn't ordered, wasn't for me. I hated my job, but without a growth mind-set, I was, in many senses, still lost at sea. Eventually, I ended up working for a very small business as a marketing assistant. Here I met two other lads and it so happened we all 'clicked' and formed a team. As a unit, we were fantastic, and over the course of five years we increased the size of the business fivefold, but our efforts were never fully acknowledged, or rewarded by the owner. We were constantly told our great ideas were 'rubbish', which was hardly motivating. If it had just been me, I would've walked out, straight into another dead-end job.

However, I wasn't on my own. We were an ideas-generating dynamo and we'd discovered we shared similar ambitions. We wanted to be the best at what we did and we wanted to succeed, but our current employment offered us little, or no, opportunities of achieving that. At this point I discovered my own growth mind-set and a similar set of values that were shared with like-minded people. Eventually we asked ourselves, 'Why are we doing this for so little return?', and so we took a leap of faith and decided we'd do it for ourselves instead. We quit and set up on our own. We invested £2,000 each of our own money into our business and bought some equipment from Italy for £6,000. We sold that to a Japanese client for £15,000. To our amazement, we were up and running, and our initial success fed our hunger to win again.

Over the following years, we sold over £150m worth of product. I attribute this success to our growth mind-set and openness to opportunities. We created a business mainly from thin air on the back of having great ideas. We focused on our goals and recognised the value of learning from our mistakes, as well as learning from the success of others. We eventually sold that business and built a multi-million-pound scale-up drone business, as well as migrating into the property market. That was possible only because we embarked on a learning pathway and because each of us was humble enough to admit that the more we learn there's yet still more to learn. No huge egos were required.

Yes, good fortune intervened, and I was lucky to be in the right place at the right time to stumble upon my future business partners. Until that moment, we'd all felt lost in some shape or form. Despite the fact we each had our own social network of friends who on Friday nights would go to the pub to 'give it large', in reality we were trapped in our own small worlds, feeling lonely and alone.

Kick-start your learning curve

Imagine what your bigger picture could be. If you're a sole trader, or a small business owner, it can feel lonely. That doesn't mean you're alone. Hundreds of amazing and diverse small business owners like you face similar issues as your own, but together, we all share similar experiences and we can all learn from each other.

If you follow my advice in Chapter 1, you'll never tell yourself again that you 'don't have time' to learn. In the next chapter, I'll explain how to apply learning and turn it into opportunities. At the end of the book I've listed some learning resources (networking groups, books, podcasts and audiobooks) that I personally found useful on my own learning pathway. Whatever issue your business is facing at this moment, it's been faced before, it's been dealt with and it's been overcome. The one thing standing in the way of your future success could simply be you.

3
Opportunities

When I tell people that it's perfectly possible (and OK) to reinvent the wheel, I'm often met with a set of blank looks. That's because we're fed the lie that you *can't* or *shouldn't*, especially when it comes to business. Without a growth mind-set, the default position is to accept failure, be that during an economic downturn, or when the orders have dried up, or if you simply don't know which way to turn and you feel stuck. In this chapter, I want to encourage you to dig deeper and explore that growth mind-set I've talked about already, because no matter what's holding you back right now, I want you to be able to turn obstacles into opportunities – and then grow. This isn't such a radical, impossible idea to get to grips with since plenty of businesses have pulled it off with great success, my own included.

The truth is, just because you've been doing something in a certain way since the year dot, that doesn't mean it's the only way, or the best way, to do it, especially if your order book is looking empty. This is when your growth mind-set will come into its own. For example, a handbag is a handbag – it's a useful accessory for carrying things around, so how come top fashion labels seem to have no problem shifting large quantities of them at £1,000 a piece versus Dave's handbags on his stall at a fraction of the price? The difference is in the *articulation* of the product. The fashion houses have turned an everyday item into a 'must have', luxury product because they've reinforced its value in the minds of customers. You might not be selling handbags, but the principles remain the same, and by the end of this chapter you'll know why. All you need is the capacity to take a step back and look objectively both at what you offer, and also at what your customers really *want*. Then you can determine if that's based on a need or a desire, and what are their 'pain points' in purchasing from you are.

Then take the 'triple R' test to:

- Re-evaluate

- Repurpose

- Reassign

Be better informed and prepared to 'reinvent' your portfolio of products, or services. It initially might seem counterintuitive, but the results of this exercise can often be surprising, with equally surprisingly simple solutions. You've got nothing to lose. Often, once business owners in a rut have taken the triple R test, they realise that the answer is right under their noses. What's previously blocked them is the fact they've been spending too much time *in* their business, rather than *on* their business. It's an insight I and my business partners were quick to learn during the credit crunch of 2008.

Re-evaluate

The credit crunch could have been the end of our business except for one thing – our growth mind-set. This told us that, in fact, this could be an opportune moment to re-evaluate our whole proposition, to repurpose our product range and to reassign its value to our customer base.

Principally, we were in the business of selling gas detection systems. The calibration consumables associated with the product were previously seen as a necessary evil. In reality, these pressurised gas cylinders were a nightmare to sell, because they were hazardous cargo items intended for customers' ships in the far corners the world. We always knew this presented us with problems, but until we were forced into examining what those problems were, we buried our heads in the sand and ignored them, because that was the easy option. It never occurred to us that the whole process also proved painful to our customers (and our competitors). Having been forced to look at those problems through our customers' eyes, I set about finding a simpler solution, that would not only serve our own customers (and ourselves) but also create an opening to serve our competitors' customers as well. It was time to reinvent the wheel (or in this case, the gas cylinder). The solution we arrived at involved using exactly the same products but marketed, managed and sold in an entirely new and frictionless way.

Repurpose

The solution (our 'FASTCALGAS') was simple: we reviewed our product portfolio and linked all the part numbers to our customers' different gas detector model names, making it simple to identify and match the correct gas to the myriad of gas detectors on the market. We averaged out hazardous carriage costs, alleviating the need for shippers to take two days to come back with a quote. We provided a world-wide guide to ports and generated an instant price guide based on the number of cylinders, which we input into a spreadsheet. As a result, we identified our 'minimal viable product' (MVP). It wasn't perfect at the start, but it was a million miles better than anything that had gone before. We created a streamlined, integrated process which, from placing the order through to delivery, was fast, efficient and seamless. In retrospect, it should have been obvious, but at that time there was no industry standard practice for ordering such parts. Each supplier used their own, chaotic system and, as a result, it actually drove all of our combined customers nuts. As was typical at the time, nobody was listening to the concerns of customers who really had to work hard at buying what they needed. However, our radical, but incredibly simple, new approach meant that our product indexing against parts and needs immediately reduced customers' purchasing efforts.

Our second initiative was to simplify the shipping costs. Instead of preparing specific quotes, we calculated the average price per route that included a built-in margin, but on which we would assume the risk if we were under. Thirdly, we reorganised our own internal distribution by arranging with our suppliers to hold stocks near the major airports. For the first time, we had fully engaged with our customers' pain points and established how to serve them best. It took the potentially business-busting credit crunch to turn us around. Come the downturn in the global market, we took that unexpected turn of events, flipped it on its head, and found a new way to exploit it. In one stroke we removed our customers' pain points of trying to match the right products to their needs, as had been standard industry practice. The FASTCALGAS model gained *massive* traction almost immediately, with customers falling over themselves to buy from us and competitors falling over themselves to try and find out what we were doing. Within two years of implementation, our FASTCALGAS product line had hit £2m per annum alone. We'd discovered a unique selling point (USP) within our niche marketplace which we then set out to own, in a similar way, for example, to Volvo owning the reputation for manufacturing the 'safest cars'. In reality, their vehicles are no different to many of their competitors, but they claimed the ground in terms of safety. We claimed the territory of saving customers both time and money, even though our products were no different to those supplied by our competitors.

What will you grab as being your own? If Greggs can do this with the sausage roll, then so can you (possibly not with a sausage roll but who knows!). Could you repurpose a product by simply taking another look at it and asking:

- What does the customer want?

- How can I articulate this without even changing anything?

- What features can I accentuate?

- Can I accessorise it to gain an advantage?

The learning curve for us at the time was the realisation that opportunities don't just exist during upturns, but that quite often they crop up during downturns, but only if you have the right mind-set to exploit them. Once you have that mind-set, you'll notice opportunities all around you and there's no need to be 100% in magpie mode where you chase every shiny object.

When an opportunity presents itself to you, establish a process that places it at the top of your sales funnel (see Chapter 10), set the criteria through which it can be filtered and apply the 'hedgehog' theory, a fantastic tool that Jim Collins adapted and refined in his excellent book, *Good to Great* (2001). In this, Collins (who adapted his theory from an ancient Greek parable in which a hedgehog outsmarts the predatory fox) states that businesses are more likely to succeed when they identify the one thing they do best. I learned a huge amount in reading this book (I recommend it to you, heartily). Collins says that when the going gets tough, it's those businesses that concentrate their efforts on what they're good at who survive and thrive. It's a theory we've adapted for our own purposes, with full acknowledgement that Collins was the inspiration. We call it the 'VAP process':

- Vision – measure it: is it met in full?

- Ability – can we be the leader in the field?

- Profit – will it make us money?

Once you apply these questions to any new opportunity, you'll know if it's an opportunity worth pursuing. If it doesn't get past all of the above, it will go nowhere and my advice is don't waste any more time on it. This process of 'opportunity filtration' is essential because the last thing you need is to grab every opportunity and run with each and every one. One problem, I believe, prevalent in British small industries is that they develop and create too many products without properly identifying in advance if there's a viable market for them, leaving them with an inventory that nobody wants to buy. However, with some careful (and inventive) repurposing, that scenario could open up a whole new set of opportunities.

It worked for champagne. As legend has it, in what looked like a fermenting disaster way back in 1693, as the Benedictine monk Dom Perignon was desperate to rid the abbey's wine of the bubbles that were deemed undrinkable. He tasted the brew on the off chance and, to his surprise, it set his head alight. 'Am I drinking the stars?' he exclaimed to the other monks he then gathered around him to taste it for themselves. And so, a whole year's grape harvest that was on the verge of being poured into the river (along with much of the abbey's potential profits) became the basis for what is now the world's best-known luxury drink, and the rest is history.

Reassign

At the end of any meeting I have with a client, I always finish up by asking them, 'Is there anything else *new* that you're looking at?' I call this the 'hidden opportunity process' – HOP. That's how we, as a business operating in the maritime industry, managed to diversify into one of the UK's leading commercial drones businesses. We did it by spotting an opportunity and reassigning our resources. In 2015, when we were looking to diversify in light of the new technologies sprouting up around us, I was in Singapore for a week having a meeting with a large oil tanker company and our Far East area manager. After we'd concluded our agenda together, I asked the question, 'What *new* technologies are you looking at?' They replied, 'What are you doing with drones?' To be honest, I knew nothing at all about some toy that, to my mind, only geeks flew around.

However, a week later and back in the UK, I had just concluded a meeting in the less exotic Wolverhampton with the West Midlands Fire Service and I asked the same question. Once again, 'drones' was the response. Now, on each occasion I could have told myself that my business was based in the maritime and safety sectors and that there was no obvious connection between these and drones. However, my growth mind-set told me otherwise because it tapped into my entrepreneurial brain. 'Watch this space' was my immediate reply. We'd never wanted to be defined by our products alone, but rather by how we could grow, both as a business and as people. Suddenly in quick succession there had been two separate occasions when an opportunity presented itself to me and, let's be honest, it wasn't hard to connect the dots. Drones was a new and emerging market that had yet to fully identify itself. I took that thought away and over the next eight months I researched the market and put it to the test. We passed the concept through our 'hedgehog'-adapted VAP process. To reiterate:

- Vision – measure it: is it met in full?

- Ability – can we be the leader in the field?

- Profit – will it make us money?

One of the most convincing answers we agreed on was that, even though we might not have specialist drone technology knowledge or experience, the principal proposition we were being asked to provide was based on increased safety – and as business providers in that field, we had that in spades. Therefore, it wasn't such a big leap for us in terms of our business-to-business (B2B) service provision and our skills were eminently transferable. The fact that our existing customers, with whom we had established a reputation for excellence already, were making noises about this new area was an opportunity we would have been foolish to ignore. Especially after we'd worked out that it could also be a highly profitable extension to our current business. After this, I wrote a business plan and showed it to the bank, who loved it and supported us. We created a new company, Coptrz, that would work in tandem with our existing one, Martek. This was the result of a HOP, and three years later the business had already sold £7m in products, training and services and was bound for the Fast Track 100.

The reason it worked was because within the space of a week I'd asked the question, probably a dozen times, 'Is there anything else *new* you're looking at?' and among the drab responses, we hooked a whale. Now imagine how the HOP could transform your own business, and the potential opportunities it could create, with minimal effort. For example, if you have ten salespeople in the field who, between them, already make a minimum of fifty calls each per day and they're finishing each call with 'What else *new* are you looking at?', how many potential opportunities might this create by just having that one simple HOP? With a growth mind-set, you are equipped to learn what's needed to diversify and grow while drawing on your core skills and reputation. No matter which pole you're sitting at, the upturn or the downturn, opportunities always exist in both hemispheres; when the horizon appears to be negative, there's usually a positive. You only have to look to nature itself for proof positive of that – wildfires fuelled by long periods of drought devastate forests and bush, but the resultant ash nourishes the soil that then grows more life.

The easier option, when you're stuck or facing a downturn, is to give up or remain static, repeating the same old patterns, including trying to be all things to everybody, which in reality will lead you nowhere. I'm guessing that's not the reason why you're reading this book – which could be the first opportunity you've created for yourself.

Take a good look at your business and what you've spent so much time, effort and resources in building. Put yourself through the 'triple R' test, do it rigorously and with complete honesty. Face the brutal facts head on and don't allow them to intimidate you. Look at what your competitors are offering. Ask yourself, 'Does the need still exist for my business?' If the answer to that is still 'yes', then go on to ask, 'How can I develop that opportunity and make it grow?' Because, assuming there's still a need for your business, then your journey isn't over. In fact, this could be a huge opportunity for you to eclipse anything you've ever done before. If you're now confident that you can pass the 'triple R' test, think of ways in which you can re-evaluate, repurpose and reassign your products, core skills and services.

Invest in the results with total enthusiasm to enable the opportunities to grow and prosper. Don't lose sight of the fact that you had the ability to start your business in the first place, because that should already tell you that you have the ability to grow.

4

Navigating a Course

Even when I was already about three years into our first business, I would run a mile from any jargon that sounded like over-the-top Americanisms. You know the type of phrases I mean: 'vision', 'strategic planning', 'mission statements' and so on. I thought these were nonsensical, soft, meaningless verbiage; Californian waffle that I couldn't relate to, invented by bangle-wearing, perfectly formed people who ate nothing but nuts and berries, sipping on their coconut water. Corporate tripe, it was money for old rope, wasn't it? But as I matured, I have to admit that my perspective began to shift.

Thinking about it, I realised I'd never get into a car without knowing where I was heading for, simply in the hope that I'd miraculously end up at the right destination. The more I sensed that it's actually a lot harder to ascertain whether you're succeeding (or not) in business if you don't know what the destination is, my 'let's drive' and 'are we there yet?' attitude began to slide away. The truth is, when we started out, we hadn't got a clue where we were going with the business. We set off aimlessly, not tracking our progress, with no sense of direction, and were in danger of ending up in a ditch with a flat tyre and no rescue service to hand. You'd have thought that after all my years at sea I'd know enough not to set off like a ship without a sail. In retrospect, we were enjoying cruising along on the crest of a wave and the perks on the top deck, but like the *Titanic,* nobody was prepared for the iceberg ahead. In our case (and many like us, to be fair), that was of course the economic crash of 2008. It was a seminal moment in my business development.

The looming disaster made me grow up and focus. It made me realise that, until then, we'd had it easy – and it *was* easy in many respects because it's not difficult to flog your goods and services when the market is as buoyant as it was prior to 2008. We didn't really have to try to sell that cleverly or work very hard, because it was a sellers' market. Anybody can run a business when other people throw their money at it, which they were doing. Demand outstripped supply, but when the crash happened, almost overnight, everything changed. That's when it really hit home for me. It was the moment I sat up and took notice of all that 'namby-pamby' jargon I'd been so quick to dismiss.

The one thing I had learned was that when adversity strikes, opportunity knocks. However, because I'd not engaged with some real fundamentals of running a business, I had no idea of what our vision for the company was, where indeed we were heading for, or what were the ramifications for our employees, ourselves included, who also happened to be shareholders. Suddenly, we were asking ourselves some pretty basic but meaningful questions for the first time:

- What do we really do?

- What service do we offer to the market?

- Who and what are we as a business?

- Where are we trying to go to?

- How do we lead our people to get there?

To survive, we certainly knew that we needed to create a definite plan of sorts because right now, life was tough and not as it had been. Our ship was sinking and we needed a plan of how to get back to the shore in order to survive. We needed to define our 'vision', 'mission' and 'values', not just for our own benefit, but for our staff too. It no longer sounded like jargon, it was a handy lifebelt dressed up in language I still couldn't really fathom, so reluctantly (but with my growth mind-set slowly developing) we looked for help. I, and my business partners, found that help in business mentorship groups, including the likes of the C-level mentorship programme called Vistage.

Unbeknown to me at the time, Vistage was a global organisation that provided a business mentorship programme with not only its own experts – each group also includes twelve business leaders or 'C-level' executives from within its local community. The group members were people just like me, ones that I could relate to, with whom each month I could share the business challenges we faced and receive feedback which prompted deep thinking and introspection and provided the space in which to grow. I began to fully engage with the concepts of 'vision', 'mission' and 'values' because, at the time, I couldn't give anyone a cogent answer when asked to describe them. The realisation for me was fourfold:

1. Up until that point I'd been arrogant and somewhat stupid.

2. I was appreciating more the value of mentorship.

3. I could no longer ignore finding ways of articulating what were our vision, mission and values.

4. More than ever in tough times you must invest in yourself and see the value not the cost.

The Vistage mentoring meetups also inspired me to work on my own personal development, something else that I'd previously thought was simply a waste of my valuable time (and money), but in fact, when I saw it as an investment in myself (which would also then have beneficial payoffs for the business), I began to connect the dots. That's why I understand the small business owners I mentor today are like I was in 2008 – they feel lost at sea and need encouragement to invest in their 'soft' skills so that they can see the bigger picture beyond the nuts and bolts of their business. For me, mentorship and personal development were the best investments I'd ever made, partly because they demystified concepts that seemed alien to this Yorkshire lad but more importantly because they made sense. Once I made sense of them, my path ahead became much clearer and my goals were easier to achieve. I realised that I had to be humble and that I didn't know everything. The truth is, millions of people have gone before us, done that and worn the T-shirt, and their experiences, successes and failures all count. And that's why we have vision, mission and values. Unpacking the jargon and explaining it in clear, relatable terms is, therefore, an excellent entry point to help us navigate the course ahead.

Vision

A simple vision statement:

> We want to double our output within two
> years and be known as the best in our region.

Vision is *not* just about your customers.

Vision is a forward-looking statement intended to inspire and give direction to your staff about where you're heading as a business. For example, the vision of a football team is to win and so it does all it needs to in order to achieve those wins (and trophies) – recruitment, skills training, good management, etc. If a football team consisted only of a group of players who simply kicked the ball about without realising that they needed to score more goals than the opposition, then it would lack vision and have zero chance of being successful.

Vision evolves from having a clear head and goes hand in hand with having a growth mind-set and working on your personal development. Stop being afraid, or cynical; engage with these concepts since they'll complement and enhance your business development. If your barriers to these are holding you back then you'll not move forward. I'm not suggesting you start shouting 'Yee ha, awesome man!' and high fiving the printer photocopier repair man. If you need to, re-read the earlier chapter on developing your growth mind-set because it's as good a starting point as any in order to prepare yourself for tackling your vision. If you need to, think of it in this way: when you're running your own business, ultimately it's a reflection of you and what you stand for, not only for your employees, but also for your suppliers and, yes, your customers at large. If you're still thinking that vision, mission and values are a whole heap of baloney, can you truly explain what they mean and why you dismiss them out of hand?

Our current company vision is to make £3m net profit before interest and taxes (EBIT) by 2023. How did we arrive at that figure? That's our aspiration based on looking at the current value of our enterprise in conjunction with the rest of our staff who participate in our share scheme. We have a very specific enterprise value we all want to reach and we've all bought into that process and goal. It wasn't a figure we plucked out of thin air, it was the result of some serious management consultation and analysis of similar companies in our sector. Understanding what our end goal was enabled us to predict the future value of the business. However, you need to start somewhere, so my first piece of advice would be to ask yourself:

1. What is your end goal? It might be to create a business for life that becomes a legacy for your children and that's then something you can begin to build your vision around. The important point to bear in mind is that vision can change according to the dynamics of the marketplace. Also, it considers how you and your business are evolving, so you don't need to stress yourself out by trying to peer into a crystal ball to see what lies ahead in twenty years. Instead, this is broken down into more manageable chunks of three or five years.

2. What are you seeking to achieve? This could take weeks, or even months, of introspection and debate to define. However, your personal end goals might be similar to the following:

- To establish the value of the business with a view to an eventual exit

- To draw a passive income where you're not hands-on in the business

- To work part-time

- To earn £0.5m a year and jump out of bed every morning ready for the fight

You will have to translate this into a vision that your staff can all get behind, because you earning £0.5m a year probably won't float their boat. No matter what your goals are, you'll be more likely to achieve them if you communicate your vision to your employees through extensive and clear communication that resonates with them. Will your vision motivate people on a daily basis and is it simple enough for people to get behind in different departments? It doesn't need to be complex. Your goal might be to achieve 500,000 active customers within a realistic timeframe, but equally your focus could be geared towards improving sales, creating effective marketing, having a reputation for the best customer service, or making positive and impactful adjustments to your administration. In fact, all departments can work towards objectives and key performance indicators (KPIs) on a quarterly basis that relate to each other, so they can measure what success looks like. The important point is that, through consultation, their buy-in to your vision is key to your successful outcome.

From the feedback you receive you can then discuss in detail with your management team how to achieve that vision. If for any reason you don't already have a management team in place, I advise you to put such a team together without further delay. You'll not be able to grow and win without one.

Vision is the bedrock of any business and the kick-start to any that finds itself lingering in the doldrums. If, like me, you've now come around to thinking what the vision for your business is, then your growth mind-set is already looking healthier than when we started. Remember, ask yourself what your desired end goal is, but take time to reflect on what your vision *might* be. Even if you do have a strong inkling, you still need some quiet reflection time because if it's wrong and you're not truthful, then everything else that follows won't work. Think big and be brave.

Mission

I've struggled with the term 'mission' in the past, mainly because there is, in my opinion, some over-intellectualised, utter rubbish that has been written about what mission is. Sometimes books conflate vision and mission, which then makes it more difficult to understand and extrapolate meaning. My straight-forward understanding, on the other hand, arises from my separation of the two terms:

- Vision is where you want to get to

- Mission is how to get there

It's not that clever. For example, if your vision is travelling to New York, you'll ask yourself, 'Where will I get the money from?', 'How long will it take to get the money?', 'Will I fly, or take a ship?' and 'Where will I book my tickets?' Answering these questions forms your mission for the vision 'DESTINATION NEW YORK'. It's all very well knowing that you want to reach New York, but not if you don't know how you'll get there. There's nothing fluffy in thinking about your mission in these terms and the same applies to your business. It's about evaluating what you need to do in order to realise vision. When I explain the differences between our current business vision and its mission, it looks like this:

- Our vision: our end goal is to make £3m net profit by 2023.

- Our mission: we'll revolutionise our customers' organisations by helping them to utilise drones to operate faster, and more safely and cheaply.

In simple terms, that means that our mission needs to tie in with the end goal. In respect of our customers, such as the emergency services, there are huge advantages in them being able to use drones. For example, a police force can now launch a drone with thermal imaging capability in a missing person hunt at a fraction of the cost per hour compared to using a helicopter. Also, drones are less likely to be grounded due to poor weather conditions or technical reasons, unlike a conventional chopper. We've also targeted civil engineering and utility companies that are saving significant sums by using our drones. One reported that they saved £750k in six months with a single drone supplied by Coptrz. Therefore, by focusing on customers who are ready to adopt drones, they reap the advantages we provide. That also means we'll not chase new prospects where there's no call for drones and where our mission to revolutionise an organisation using drones is a redundant proposition. We don't spend time chasing clients that have no need for our services, and that in turn makes us more efficient, and ultimately more profitable. It's how we're growing our company quickly in line with our vision. We're not wasting time on people who are not in that buying mode, because not doing so will make us efficient, more profitable and able to grow the business quickly.

Values

Values are what really underpin a business. Having a set of values that everyone in the business adheres to is the most important element of all.

I'll be blunt. You might have a worked out a brilliant vision and you've nailed your mission, but if your business is populated by a bunch of w*****s who don't share, or give a s**t, about your values, then you might as well forget it. You'll never achieve your goals. This applies to any size business, be it a small workshop on the outskirts of town or a mega-rich business in a glass-fronted office block in a city centre.

Let me give you an example. I was talking with the CEO of a multi-million-pound business that simply wasn't growing, it was stagnating. It was obvious that in the near future, its competitors would have the edge and the business would be in trouble, issuing profit warnings with all the resultant upheaval that would cause internally. On paper, the business should have been expanding, but for some reason its vision wasn't happening. It wasn't until the CEO took a closer look inside the business that he discovered where the problem lay, and that was with the sales director. Irrespective of the fact that this person was absolutely killing their targets each month, he acted more like a 'lone wolf', constantly working against everyone in his team and lacking any sort of rapport with his colleagues. Nobody could get on with him because of his arrogant and abrasive working practices and, as a result, staff performance around him was extremely poor. The CEO took a very brave and scary decision to fire his star performer and guess what? Staff morale and performance improved overnight and dramatically so. The key lesson was that the business had found it was stuck because its star performer wasn't aligned with its values. When a business has a 'cancer' within, then it needs to be cut out, pronto. Over the next five years this business leapt forward with the CEO buoyed by the realisation that 'people values' were everything and the business has since achieved a valuation at the last count of over £1bn.

The question is, how does a business establish exactly what its values are? The answer is, it takes time working them out. Don't be concerned if values are not always apparent when you start a company from scratch. It wasn't until just over two years into our latest venture in the drone business, after we'd established a trading history, that we really began to think about what it was that we stood for as a business. We approached our original and newly recruited staff and asked them, 'What do we stand for? What makes us great, what's good about us?' After a while we distilled all the feedback into three things. To this day, we signpost these (abbreviated to 'GOLD') on the walls of our offices so that our values are embedded into the working day from the moment we arrive, to long after we leave:

GOLD

1. **Grow:** we're always learning, but we're also a training business. If for any reason we lose sight of our growth mind-set, then we've gone seriously wrong. We know our staff all perform better if they grow, and so we always aim to stretch ourselves and to go outside of our comfort zones.

Our mantra, therefore, is to just be curious and to continually learn – otherwise our business won't grow.

2. **Outwork** the competition: 'outwork' was a term that our employees felt reflected how we stand out from the crowd. We work hard and we try harder. It's also about thinking big in what we're doing, being resilient, consistent and relentless. It's not about working sixteen hours a day, but about doing the things that count. Personally, I get out of bed at 5am and I think to myself 'I bet my competitors aren't doing this' and I use this time on personal development.

3. **Leverage:** we utilise the art of leverage to multiply our output by using outworkers, groups and partnerships.

4. **Disrupt:** we're inventive, ingenious and trailblazing. We now ask ourselves every day, 'Are we disrupting the market? Are we being brave enough to be inventive, ingenious and trailblazing with what we do?' We're not in business to do the same as other companies, so if they do A, we'll do B, plus C. Discovering new ways of doing business and disrupting the market is so important to us. As is the flexibility to know that if things don't turn out right, then we're prepared to fail, not get hung up about it. If we fail in something, we might tweak our approach slightly, but if it fails again, we quickly move on.

It's us being brave enough to stay several jumps, not just one, ahead of our competitors. We're not afraid to put a few people's backs up, not because we're arrogant or adversarial, but because we like to find out who's really listening to us: whose attention have we grabbed? Because they're our valuable, niche market, we don't have to (or want to) please the whole market the whole of the time. Our demographic is the minority. If we tried to serve everybody, we'd serve nobody. Being brave helps us grow, because out of half a dozen new initiatives, four might not cut it, but two might just catch on. No point in flogging dead horses.

That's what having stated values means to our business. Without these, we'd stop growing. As a priority in any of our meetings about our products and services, we place our values at the top of the agenda and we ask, 'Are these products and services aligned with our values?' If they're not going to help us grow, outwork the competition, or be disruptive, then they're no longer on the agenda. And the more you embed those values, the more you live them and the more you work them, the bigger your success will be.

Your vision, mission and values needn't be complicated, wordy or pretentious – plain and simple and to the point is ideal. For example, here is the values and mission statement of the fish-and-chip shop chain Harry Ramsden's – it's straight-talking and to the point:

'To be the best loved Fish & Chips business by offering the best Fish & Chips and best dining experience you can buy at great value.'

You'll notice that this statement encapsulates in only a few words everything the business believes in terms of its quality and service delivery.

Thinking about your own vision, mission and values statement, what will your customers, suppliers and employees learn about you when they read it?

5
Strategy

For some, the term 'strategy' is more of a stigma than a business tool and is best avoided because it has that stink of corporate bad breath hanging over it. I should know, because that used to be me back in the day when I thought that 'strategy' was the preserve of only the educated and their intellectual neural pathways. It certainly wasn't for the likes of me, having left school with just a few exam results under my belt, and little else. After all, I'd still been able to work my way up and improve my lot by running a business with my co-partners without a fancy set of letters after my name, so why did I need any such thing called strategy? To a certain extent that was true – our business in the 2000s was performing well and we were turning over a healthy revenue with clients all over the world. We didn't really have a plan, we just wanted to make money, and more of it, and that's exactly what we did. Until the financial crash in 2008, when our business ground to a halt. It wasn't until then that, better late than never, we realised that if we were going to ride out this storm, we needed a plan. Or, in other words, a strategy.

Quite why I'd never made that link – between a strategy and a plan being more or less the same thing – I can only attribute to the fact that I'd always dismissed jargonistic words as irrelevant to my own experience or aspirations. It never occurred to me that it was just another term for an activity that I carried out in my everyday life all the time – such as planning a car journey. This needs a well-maintained car of the right size to fit the required passengers, with enough funds to pay for the return journey; the tank needs filling with the right fuel type, and the route needs plotting and the journey times calculated to ensure an appropriate arrival time. It's exactly the same in business if your aim is to become a market leader.

Developing a strategy

At this point I accept that you're keen to get to grips with formulating your own strategy and wondering who can best mentor you by sharing their advice and experience. In my case, for our drones business, I and my partners knew we wanted it to be an innovative enterprise that embraced technology. We'd always been forward-looking and because we identified an opportunity, just as our traditional maritime business was maturing, we began by investigating various concepts that formed the 'internet of things', or 'IoT' as it's known. That entailed me researching what was out there and attending numerous high-tech conferences in San Francisco and wondering how the hell anybody ever sold anything because everybody only seemed to sell 'concepts' and ran for cover when I tried to talk commercials. However, one of those concepts was drones, which immediately triggered my interest and desire.

The consumer market for drones was already growing nicely but it occurred to me that on a commercial level there were very few early adopters in a potentially significant and, as yet, untapped market. Reporting this back to my partners and by employing the VAP process I described in Chapter 3, backed up by encouraging forecast studies conducted by the likes of PwC and Goldman Sachs, we recognised that this could potentially be an amazing opportunity. Our strengths lay in our B2B product and service skills and, on that basis, we saw no reason why we couldn't become the biggest commercial supplier of drones in the UK and Ireland to start with. Together with our already established international reputation, we also set our sights on becoming the biggest in the world. However, following careful consideration, given that we were a relative newcomer into the market and a small operation, we agreed that we should refocus our goal to be the No. 1 in the UK and Ireland. Globally the market is worth $154bn so being the dominant player in the fifth biggest economy within five years from launch was still an extremely attractive and ambitious proposition. What's more, our refocused strategic thinking made that ambition more achievable. Part of that refocusing was based on analysing what we would have required (as fuel) to become world No. 1, such as the extra funding, thus increasing our risk and exposure. Plus, the thought was in our minds that if we tried to serve everybody, we'd serve nobody. It taught us that one of the big advantages of strategic planning, using the hedgehog test and our VAP process, is the ability to know from the outset what *not* to do. While the VAP results showed us we might not be able to be best in the world at selling drones, we could, however, be the best on our home turf. It also confirmed our instinct that, based on our B2B expertise, we shouldn't try to enter the business-to-consumer (B2C) marketplace, despite that sector showing a healthy growth in demand and sales. We then further refined the strategy by ruling out targeting commercial photography and videography for the film and TV industry because that was already a relatively mature market (with less expensive kit). Instead, we targeted surveying, as that was an area in which we could excel, and it also attracted a high premium. We also set our sights on the emergency services and industrial safety inspections (which was also a natural fit with our background). Through our strategic planning, we had discovered our niche and had identified an achievable pathway to maximise results. Niche is good.

Therefore, if you have ever struggled, as I once did, with the notion of creating a strategy, I hope that by now your fears, concerns and adversity towards it have been allayed. I've included a starter checklist below that will help this vital process and encourage you to focus your thoughts on your business, and how it can be most profitable by creating a strategic plan so that your business can navigate from A to B. I am the first to admit that, even to this day, occasionally the thought of strategic planning can bring me out in a cold sweat, because the questions raised always pose certain challenges. However, just like any physical journey, by road, rail, water or air, it requires a process of thinking it all through and ensuring that you're in a fit state to reach your goal. Once you can apply that analogy to your business, the term 'strategy' begins to feel more relevant – and important – to the long-term growth of your empire.

As I mentioned in Chapter 1, having a growth mind-set means that you're capable of thinking big. While others in your well-meaning family or friendship circles might think you're a dreamer with unachievable aims, take no notice. In fact, take yourself away to that quiet place again so that you can begin to rationalise your plan and piece it together, chunk by chunk. Give your thoughts the time and space to develop freely and write them down as they occur to you, until you are able to say to yourself, 'This is what I want to do.' Whether that's to be known as the best in your area or your niche, or to expand from a local business into a national concern, committing yourself to a strategic plan is key to that eventual outcome. Nor should you feel overwhelmed or alone at this point, because this is where mentorship can play a significant role which needn't cost you a penny in the first instance. Both online (such as LinkedIn) and offline networking resources offer a wide range of opportunities to reach out to business leaders who will be willing to share their advice. One of the most powerful statements I've ever heard in business is: 'I wonder if you could help me?' I've never heard anyone respond with 'no' before they hear what you want. The last place to seek advice is from friends and family – they are well meaning, as I say, but unless they share your vision, mission and values, and believe in your dream big time (and unconditionally so), then their advice could potentially trip you up at the first hurdle. They might want the best for you, but that doesn't mean to say they are best equipped to advise you on your strategy. *You* are the one with the entrepreneurial spark and it's akin to speaking a different language.

Strategic planning starter checklist

- Where are you now?

- What resources do you have?

- What skill sets does your team need?

- What do you need to fuel your expansion plans? For example, do you need to borrow funds or change your credit terms to improve your cashflow?

- How are you going to navigate towards your expansion?

- What are your marketing plans (or, where are you going to get your customers from)?

- What will your sales process be and how will you manage it?

- How will you provide customer service backup?

- What will you be selling?

- Who will you be selling to?

- What's the price structure?

- What's the intended timeframe?

6

Impact

With so much 'noise' in all business sectors across both digital and traditional channels, it's more important than ever for you to stand out over the background crackle of static. Knowing and maximising your point of difference in the eyes of your customers is key to your strategic plan's successful outcome. The days when businesses could sit back on their laurels and rely on a regular stream of customers, limited by their choices of supplier, are long gone. These days, it pays (yes, it's essential) to be 'disruptive', another one of those jargon terms that has crept its way into the business world's lexicon. I can fully understand why many people find it an ugly or unwanted term, but the truth is, if you're an entrepreneur looking to scale up your business, if you're not seen as a disruptor, or disrupting the status quo in some way, then you might as well pack up and go home. If you're not making enough noise these days, then the world will simply pass you by.

Therefore, you must recalibrate your thinking about the word 'disrupt' and destigmatise it. What it tells us is that in business you need to be seen differently by your customers, but what worries many of the SME business owners that talk to me is how they learn to be disruptive. Some feel that it's not in their nature, but that's because they mistake the word as being the same as 'aggressive' or 'rude'. It's not, and furthermore, we're all born disruptive when we scream for our mother's attention wanting to be fed. As children growing up, we're not inhibited by social norms because we don't know what they are, and we inherently understand that to get what we want, we need to disrupt the status quo by making an impact on those whose attention we seek. If we hold onto our natural childlike abilities to disrupt and ignore our learned, preconceived ideas about what other people think about us, we can begin to re-learn how to make an impact.

That means we need to stand out more, and as a consequence, we must be prepared to be criticised. For some, that's a difficult notion to embrace because of perhaps painful childhood memories where criticism manifests itself through bullying, maybe because they didn't fit in at school. However, this is not about the way you feel, it's about business and it's not personal. Once people begin to criticise you, it shows they're taking an interest in you and for that to happen you need to make some changes if you want to make an impact. It's one of the most difficult things for many business owners to accept when they see their competitors conducting their own businesses in standardised ways. That being so, they ask me, why do they need to change? My response is, look at how Eddie Stobart disrupted the logistics and haulage sector, by using distinctively coloured trucks which each bore a woman's name, to the extent that the business became a household name and a media favourite. His move to rebrand his vehicles was essentially a disruptive one in what was, quite frankly, a dull market of grey or black diesel-guzzlers and pollution emitters. Stobart realised that to stand out he needed to embrace change. In general, people don't like, and are scared of, change. Stobart proved them wrong and his actions saw him scale his business from a small fleet of Carlisle-based vehicles to a national entity with more than 2,200 on the road.

Challenge yourself and dream

Disruption, therefore, needn't be an aggressive change, it can simply be doing things differently to everyone else. If you believe in what you're doing and that fits with your strategy and your vision, then see it as an opportunity and embrace the fact that you *are* different. It doesn't matter that not everybody will like it: you can be sure that as soon as people start commenting about and criticising you, suddenly you'll reach terminal velocity. In all probability, more people will sit up and take notice and like what they see (as opposed to those that don't), and many will jump ship and climb on board as your supporters and fans. With so much choice available to customers in the globalised marketplace, having a clear point of difference compared to your competitors raises your profile above the noise that is filled with a myriad of other products, just like yours. Do your homework and research what your competitors' businesses look like in the eyes of the customer, but don't be tempted to simply tweak a product or service if essentially it's still the same as every other in the marketplace. To really stand out, challenge yourself and ask: what if you made your product, or provided your service, in a completely different way to everyone else? By adding a point of difference to your offering, your business can both disrupt, and capture, the attention of the market because it stands out from the crowd.

Nor do you have to be of Uber-sized proportions to realise the aspirations of the business. With your growth mind-set feeding your vision, mission and values, which are then aligned to your strategy, it's possible to disrupt and create impact in almost any traditional sector. Disrupting can mean many things and doesn't need a new invention. It could be as simple as changing the colour of your fleet of delivery vehicles from black to pink – that would certainly make your business stand out! Don't allow your mind to think of disruption as a negative thing. More importantly, be prepared for the fact that no matter what, some people will always criticise you, especially as you become more successful. In my opinion, criticism in many ways is a good thing. You're making people face their own insecurities because they're not achieving what you are. Instead, allow yourself to think differently and enjoy those lightbulb moments. Allow yourself to dream and then take time to learn from your customers what they want and what they don't want. Engage with them to discover what their frustrations and complaints are, since feedback of this nature is a gift to you and your business. In responding to their concerns and by improving your product, or service, you have the chance to convert those customers into your loyal ambassadors and, jointly, you could disrupt the market. When Virgin Atlantic transformed the cabin crew experience from the point of view of the customer, it was intoxicating to the market. It was still about the simple proposition of flying from A to B, except it had gone from being a functional to an experiential transaction. One 'small' shift in Virgin Atlantic's customer service delivery resulted in a massive disruption to the airline industry as a whole and, as a result, many of its competitors had to play catch-up. It reinvented the long haul flight industry that previously hadn't taken much notice of its customers' frustrations and needs. Imagine what your business could achieve with similar thinking, irrespective of its size. Nor does it matter that all of your potentially disruptive ideas work; simply be prepared to fail fast and try the next one.

If you're now more willing to give over the space and time to your growth mind-set, to spot new opportunities when the unexpected happens, identify your vision, mission and values and then your strategic path accordingly, there's no reason why your business doesn't have the capability to disrupt and scale up as a result. Dream, and be different with the intention of creating a positive impact on your customers.

7
People vs Talent

Your business is about people, it's not about you. Without good people who understand your vision, share your values and can effectively implement your mission, your business will never realise its full potential. In fact, the less you value your people and insist on running it your way, the more likely it will be to stagnate and potentially come to a complete standstill, or fail. Recruiting, training and retaining the right people is perhaps one of the biggest headaches any small business owner faces, especially if they don't fully understand what's involved. For many, it's a real bear trap, but in their haste to fill vacant positions, they rush headlong into making uninformed and knee-jerk decisions. That's especially true when recruitment demand outstrips supply, with small business owners filling a vacant seat with no more than a warm body. Nobody wins in this scenario. In this chapter I will guide you through some of the essentials – some obvious, others not – that you need to consider before you even call anyone in for interview. I'll also explain the preparation process, as well as describe how to avoid some of the commonest traps I've seen others fall into.

If you're new to business leadership and just starting out, or it's been a while and you're ready to recruit because the business is expanding, the whole hiring process can represent a huge area of unknowns. Even your past experience might not have taught you well and you've ended up spending large sums of money on agency fees or head-hunters only to end up with less than satisfactory employees despite all your efforts. If that's been a repetitive pattern, then perhaps it's trying to tell you something and it's time to sit up and take notice. For starters, the costs to the business are huge when you get it wrong, especially if that's a cycle that repeats itself over and over again. But when recruitment is done properly, there's nothing more exciting than hiring really great people who are aligned with your values and who will grow your business. Planning your recruitment strategy is, therefore, every bit as important as planning your sales and marketing.

Planning

Ultimately the vacancy you may need to fill is for the job you're doing right now. By that, I mean, you should be looking to effectively make yourself 'redundant'. That might sound daft on the surface, but when you think about it, by doing this you're armour-plating your business. Otherwise the business will always be incumbent on you, in every single area of its operations and, as a result, you will be a slave to it. That's not an ideal position to occupy if you're looking to grow your business, especially if a future sale may be in your mind, or if you're looking to create a lifestyle that allows you to spend more time away from it and on your leisure activities. Of course, if you can't tear yourself away and can't handle the thought of anyone else doing what you currently do, then so be it. You're not the type who will even consider making themselves redundant, because you're indispensable in every way and you prefer having a workforce that's more subservient, following your orders. If so, all well and good, but believe me, in my experience, your business won't grow much beyond what it is today. I can say this with confidence because I see it all the time where small business owners and sole traders are swamped by the sheer volume of day-to-day necessary tasks that need completing simply to keep the ship afloat. They might have plans to scale up, but because they can't ever see the wood for the trees, they don't have the time and space to consider how to make that a reality. It's not their fault, they just haven't been shown how.

Once again, I'll point you towards the principles I laid out at the beginning of the book – facing the brutal facts. Step aside for a while and ask yourself, 'What am I good at? What am I not good at?' Answer these questions with complete honesty and don't allow any part of your ego to interfere. It's tempting to believe that we can be good at everything we do but, in truth, that's not how humans work. Crucially, be honest about what aspects you enjoy, because otherwise it's an uphill battle to grow a business successfully if you're constantly rolling up your sleeves to do tasks you don't enjoy. Do you really want to spend the rest of your working life on jobs that give you the pip? What might be your nemesis could turn out to be another's nirvana. Recruiting that person has to be the better option, and it frees you up to focus on areas in the business that really need your attention.

Recruitment

When thinking about recruitment, you need both a strategy and a process in place so that the decisions you make are informed and valuable, and the outcomes deliver the best ROI (return on investment) for you and your business. The business in question might be the small one you're currently heading up and you need to put people in place so that you can move on. Or, you may currently be looking to expand your team because nothing seems to be working and you're finding that much of your valuable time is spent in dealing with people problems. What you are certain of is that you no longer want to be the one needing to micromanage. You know that if your business is to grow, you also need the time and space for your growth mind-set to flourish, and so hiring the right people that can serve the vision, mission and values of the business will be key to that future success. It's an issue that I see many business owners trying to grapple with and it causes more anxiety than it needs to. Over the years, we've refined our recruitment strategy and process, which beforehand was one of our biggest pain points and where we made some costly mistakes. These are the lessons I'll share below which, if you implement them as part of your own recruitment process, will be some of the most important accelerators of your business.

Talent, not just people

One of the biggest revelations we discovered was using a 'flywheel technique', a model which we adapted from Jim Collins' excellent book *Good to Great* that I've previously referenced. In essence, our version of the flywheel is divided into six segments, the first of which is labelled 'talent'. As a noun, it goes way beyond the generic term 'people'; applying that to your thinking from the outset means you're not simply looking to populate the business with bodies, but with people who have a natural aptitude, or skill, and a growth mind-set. That's a very different perspective on hiring new team members. It immediately focuses your attention towards attracting great talent into your business who can then drive it forward across different areas, such as marketing, sales, operational delivery and, yes, even accounts. If you're completely honest with yourself, although you might have been handling any one, or all, of these areas until now, can you say that you have the talent to drive them forward? Be honest and ask yourself:

- What are you good at?

- Where do you come up short?

- What tasks do you enjoy most?

- Which cause you the most pain?

For example, you might excel at finding new leads, but struggle to convert these into sales. In that case, the obvious solution will be to recruit a salesperson, but that has to be the *right* salesperson with the necessary talent. Not simply a person who can fill the position. In such a scenario, we create a tailored 'job scorecard' which is designed to achieve the stated outcomes identified prior to advertising the role.

Here is an example of pre-identified outcomes for a sales role:

- All leads to be followed up within twenty-four hours.

- Achieve a conversion rate of 50%.

- Increase gross margin from 30% to 50% within twelve months.

Unlike a traditional job description, which really only describes the role, we focus on the desired *outcomes* first so that we can build a portrait of that ideal person, what they're doing right now and where they currently are in their career path. Once we've completed that part of the recruitment planning process, then attracting their attention to us is key. In many ways, this is more about *us* selling ourselves to *them*. Therefore, we invest in short, impactful video-show reels (two or three minutes long) that tell our story: who we are, why we're a great company to work for and what our values and culture are.

In terms of marketing you and your business, video is a very powerful tool and we all have the capability of creating engaging content. You don't necessarily need video production aptitude, but you do need the right attitude in order to directly engage with the people you want to reach. Don't think that if you're a sole trader, or a small business with only a couple of employees, this won't work for you. If you have ambitions to grow, simply be honest and enthusiastic about your big plans and make it clear that you're looking to hire somebody who can take you forward. Then say what you're offering in return. If that's minimum wage and no prospects, then don't be surprised if you attract responses from people who won't be able to grow your business.

In a competitive employment marketplace you need to pull out all the stops to attract the best candidates, so it's vital you play your best cards, not simply with the remuneration and the perks, but also the working environment and the culture in which the prospective employee will find themselves. It doesn't matter how big or small your business is, the person looking at your video reel needs to feel they can engage with you and understand your vision, mission and values. If you've already engaged with the content of this book thus far, then you'll have begun to build on the emotional capital that talented people find so attractive.

At this point, if you're thinking, 'Yes, I want to do this' but you've broken into a cold sweat thinking about how you'll create and pay for a video, it's not difficult, and it's not expensive. In fact, anyone with a smartphone can record and upload their video for free. The more personal and authentic it feels, the better. Or, make use of free-to-use online platforms to create more sophisticated videos, using split screens and slides to tell your story. An example of such a platform is 'Soapbox' (https://wistia.com/soapbox). All you need to invest is a little bit of time, effort and, of course, forethought. As long as you are authentic and as presentable as possible, then a few minutes of your time is a good use of it if you want to reach the right people. If you approach it half-heartedly, however, then guess what? You'll only get back what you put in. It's worth getting out of bed that extra hour earlier to focus on your outcome of attracting the best people possible to apply for the job.

Filtering

Begin the process by nailing down your job scorecard and then composing the advert based on the outcomes. Think about how you'll market it (including video) and where to promote it. This is not an expensive process, and therefore shouldn't be a barrier to any small business. We often use platforms such a 'ZipRecruiter' and 'Indeed' which in reality cost no more than a couple of hundred pounds. The advantage is that online platforms offer you a much wider reach and more instant responses, which we then filter through our initial criteria test:

- Intelligence

- Energy

- Attitude

My thinking behind this is that if I can employ intelligent, energetic people with a real can-do attitude, we can move mountains. For example, with salespeople I'll teach them how to sell and they'll assimilate the learning and be able to apply it with little friction. We apply the filters 'IEA' to the online application process:

- **Intelligence:** when a person responds to the advert online, they receive an automatic response which asks them to complete a short intelligence test we've created. Anyone scoring below 30 automatically won't progress to the next stage.

- **Energy and attitude:** those progressing to the next stage are contacted by our virtual assistant who has been trained to rate respondents on a scale of 0 to 5. Initial observations which are assessed are:

  1. Appearance

  2. How they rate against our people values

  3. Their ability to grow

  4. Their work ethic

  5. What research they have done on us

  6. Only then, any relevant experience

From experience, by applying filters such as these, you'll be able to eliminate 50% of respondents because they won't have read the advert correctly. On average, 50% of the remaining candidates then fail the intelligence test, and again, in the next round, 50% won't progress beyond the short pre-interview.

It's only after all those filters have been applied that our virtual assistant will arrange a direct ten-minute video interview between myself and the candidate. Up until that point, much of the time and pain associated with recruitment hasn't even crossed my path, freeing me up to concentrate on the business. That's when you realise the real benefits of the process and scoring system I've described above, because otherwise you'll think, 'I like this person, they're like me.' My strongest advice to business owners: resist the natural urge to recruit in your own image.

Applying and acting on these filters is something that you can easily handle for yourself as a small business owner. As you expand and your recruitment needs become more constant, it's a responsibility that you will ultimately need to train somebody else to carry out for you. Again, this isn't prohibitively expensive and in our case we are happy to use overseas services, such as 'OnlineJobs.ph', that we confidently outsource to.

Interviewing

Having agreed to a ten-minute video interview, this is the moment when you can act upon a series of informed responses. You'll already have formed an impression of the candidate based on their scores as a result of the filtering criteria. Personally, my instinct tells me if they're going to meet those criteria within the first thirty seconds, and given that I've seen other people wasting over an hour of their precious time talking to somebody they're never going to employ, then ten full minutes of my time is an efficient use of it while maintaining credibility with any recruitment agencies that I also occasionally use. Following this, I will be quite ruthless in my selection of who I'm going to take forward. This results in up to ninety minutes of face-to-face interview when I expect the candidate to come prepared with a presentation – for which a brief has been sent in advance – on how they would intend to smash their targets if they got the job.

This is the final, most thorough part of the process since it shows you which applicant has spent meaningful time researching for the job they've applied for, as opposed to those who have cobbled together a weak presentation without giving it much serious thought. I learn a lot about the candidates' talent at this stage, and it's never solely about me making a decision based on the fact I like them, or not. Instead, it's based on the level of detail they've prepared for their presentation. From this, I can better judge whether they're a twenty-minute person, or a five-hour, focused person. I ask them searching questions to see if their responses match our values and culture, such as how they funded their time at university, or what podcasts they listen to, or what was the last business book they read. Inevitably, the candidates that respond with precise and informed answers help us to separate the wheat from the chaff. The one element that always impresses me the most is if they answer with honesty and integrity, not simply with what they think I want to hear. If they demonstrate a sincere desire to learn more than they already know, then they're coachable and we're able to tap into their growth mind-set. The fact that you will have taken all this time and effort to create and implement a process will often encourage applicants to want the job more because it's a challenge. They'll also respect you because you've thought about the interview in depth and they can see that you're both professional and serious about it, unlike simply having a chat and finishing up with, 'I like you. Here's a job.' How would they value that job then?

From your perspective, even if you're faced with a raft of candidates, you still might not find that exact person you're looking to hire. Don't be tempted, in that case, to take on the best of a bad bunch. Keep going and keep refining your criteria, because if you make the wrong decision in haste to fill the position, this *will* be very costly. The last thing you want is to find, six months down the line, that your new recruit has screwed up your relationships with clients, or they're woefully behind on reaching their targets. Then you sack them after months of angst where your subconscious is telling you 'they're just wrong for the job', and then have to go through the whole recruitment process again. In some cases, depending on the size of your business and the role that needs filling, that can cost you a pretty penny, or more. As I say, don't employ for employment's sake. If you were the manager of a football team, you'd certainly make sure you had the right players for the right positions on the pitch. You wouldn't consider fielding a defender in your striker's position. As Jim Collins says, 'The right people in the right seats, on the team bus' – and he's right.

Keep track

It's vital that you track the progress you're making with your recruitment. As a discipline, it says as much about you in terms of your own time efficiency planning as it does about the people you're recruiting. If you can't keep your house in order, the whole process will become messy and, in all likelihood, you'll employ the wrong person, or even miss the person who's just right for your business. I prefer to use an online tool, 'Trello' (www.trello.com) which is free, with premium upgrades if required. If you're not already familiar with it, take a look, run a trial and then discover how it falls into place. At any stage during the selection process I use this resource to see who's applied, been rejected or who's going forward to video interview. It's designed around project management and you should treat tracking your recruitment drive as a project – a *very* important one.

Develop and retain

Develop

Having invested time, effort and energy into your recruitment process and finding that right person, it's your job to develop and retain them. In the past, we've not been as attentive as we could have been with our inductions. Today, we see this as the first important step for the new employee's introduction to the business. Creating an induction plan is, therefore, vital. Again, using Trello (see above) to track their progress is useful as it allows both parties to cross-check that they have gone through any necessary documentation, which is then marked off as read during their probation period. We review this with them on a monthly basis.

We've also discovered that the practice of asking new recruits to send us an email at the end of every day during their first month with their response to three questions about their progress provides us with hugely beneficial insight into how they're settling in. The three questions are:

- What did you achieve today?

- What challenges did you face today?

- Have any questions arisen from today?

Answering the questions shows whether they have the discipline to carry this task out on a daily basis and at the same time keeps us informed. It's also a simple but effective means of maintaining dialogue through questions and conversation. In return, we reflect their own appetite for discipline by ensuring that we respond daily to these emails. It's a two-way street but the impact is powerful, especially in spotting where we might have made a mistake in our selection, despite all our best efforts to avoid this. Mistakes do happen – spotting them and acting upon them is, therefore, very important.

Many potential issues and misunderstandings can be mitigated against if the induction planning follows a planned structure and process. Ensuring regular probation reviews and weekly one-to-ones with a series of questions employees fill in beforehand are just as useful for the new person as they are for you. After the first four weeks, these reviews can be scheduled monthly, by which time you should be able to inform them as to where their future with your business is heading. Below are examples of questions grouped into themes that we typically ask our people.

Progress to date:

- What are you pleased with since your last review? (For example, objectives completed/over-delivery on a task/a positive change you have put in place.)

- Have you had the chance to do what you do best every day since your last one-to-one? Rate this on a scale of 1–10.

- What (if anything) has stopped you achieving a 10 on the above?

Objectives account:

- Which objectives are you not confident in achieving (be prepared to discuss recovery actions)?

- What has distracted/sidetracked you from focusing on these this month?

Opportunities and challenges:

- What key challenges are you facing at the moment?

- What can you do to overcome these challenges?

Improvement:

- What didn't you do to the best of your ability this month and what will you work on improving next month?

Commitment:

- What do you commit to undertake between now and the next one-to-one?

- What will you
  - Stop
  - Start
  - Continue?
- What specific support do you need this month?

Retain

It's all so different today than when we first started our business. We live in the time of the 'millennials' whose expectations are very different to the 'baby boomers' and 'Generation X'. For millennials, staying in the same job for two or three years is like the grass is growing under their feet, and it's our challenge to firstly attract and then to retain them. How can we do that?

First, create a personal development plan for each individual. Make the effort to learn what they're aiming for, and in response, how you can support them in achieving that. Give them objectives that stretch them and rework these on a quarterly basis. At each stage, keep track of this (for example, document it in Trello) so that you can keep returning to it during your regular one-to-ones. In our business, we also like to offer an incentive scheme whereby every employee benefits from a pooled 10% share of the business equity (known as a 'phantom share scheme'). It's a way of rewarding loyalty and achieving targets on an annual basis and it enables us to retain the talent we're privileged to work with. As and when the business is sold, each employee benefits. My aim is that all the staff who join us on our journey, and remain in our employ, will at some point in the future receive a significant six-figure sum into their current accounts and, in all probability, be able to return to work the following morning and carry on as normal, if that's what takes their fancy. It will be our way of rewarding them for helping us outwork the competition, disrupt the market and continue to grow as people. It's a self-regulating scheme as it means that everyone who works with us is accountable to the next person for the success of the business. Anyone who chooses to move on before that event occurs has their share returned to the pot.

Of course, our aim is, having recruited the right talent, to keep them all on board with us. It's why we, as leaders, are also open to scrutiny by the work-force. Every three months we conduct an employee engagement survey that tracks all feedback based on a series of scientifically derived questions designed by Gallup and disseminated via SurveyMonkey. All the feedback is anonymous and is reviewed by the management team and discussed on a quarterly basis. At times when we've fallen down with our employee engagement and our ratings have dipped, despite our best efforts, we remain open and honest about the results. We always try to find ways to put it right because we trust the level of intelligence of the talented people we were at pains to recruit in the first place. In fact, this underpins our whole philosophy of supporting our talent from the bottom up. We support this approach wholeheartedly and we cheerlead it. We're humble enough to listen to feedback, and we don't allow our egos to get in the way of ourselves. We recognise that the more we learn, the more we realise we need to learn. Therefore, perhaps we need to revisit that old phrase of 'many hands make light work' in the belief that simply hiring more people will be the solution to all our problems. Rather, we should focus on what those many hands can offer the business in terms of embracing a growth mind-set, and sharing our vision, mission and values. Putting that attitude into practice creates an exciting, forward-thinking working environment that will make all the difference between recruiting the right people to share the workload, or attracting talent to help the business grow.

8
Rhythm and Discipline

The human body is a sophisticated and complex system of interconnected nerves, tissues and organs. At its centre is the heart, triggered by a synaptic transmission from the brain by which a neuron communicates with a target cell across a synapse, every second, minute by minute, hour by hour, and day by day. Without the repeated rhythm of a heartbeat, we'd find it impossible to stay alive. As a metaphor, the heart is often (over) used to describe how we should think about our business and purpose in life. Although in my opinion, it serves to illustrate the emotional aspect of why we all do what we do.

However, if we look closer at the function of the heart, we're able to draw an even deeper comparison with running a business that marries the why with the how. The heart doesn't act in isolation, it's dependent on neurotransmitters so that it performs its function with unfailing regularity. Conversely, the brain relies on a constant oxygen supply pumped around the body by the heart, acting as the body's engine. It's a perfect, symbiotic partnership of heart and mind that keeps us all moving forward from one moment to the next, day after day. In this chapter I'll be exploring the functionality of the 'heartbeat of business' and how it can work in partnership with your own growth mindset. Together, they enable your business engine to run smoothly, efficiently and automatically. To do that, we need to think more about how we structure our daily operations so that we become accustomed to running our businesses in a structured, succinct way. The more rhythm and discipline become automatic, the more we can best drive the business forward. Just as with the heart, our business engines need fuel, and then we need to ignite it.

Meetings!

I'll be the first to admit that when I began my first business, none of this was a consideration. We were all too ready to be reactive and knee-jerk in our responses, only thinking in the moment, for the moment. It wasn't long before we realised we needed to attempt to inject some planning processes, so we began by setting meetings, because that's what was *expected* of management. They have meetings and this looks and feels really important and grown up. Except, we didn't give any thought to structuring those meetings: there were no agendas, time limits or agreements as to what the outcomes of those meetings should be. In truth, the meetings were little more than talking shops and, dare I say it, a complete waste of time which didn't drive the business forward one jot. Then it dawned on us that perhaps we ought to set our agendas and take minutes of these meetings, which perversely resulted in us setting more and more meetings than there were hours in the day. We were creating a monster and it was impossible for any of us to deliver all of the proposed outcomes. Looking back, we simply lacked discipline in how we structured and ran those very important meetings.

Fortunately, however, this coincided with the onset of our curiosity about our growth mind-set for the business. Instinctively we knew we needed to improve how we managed ourselves and our time if we wanted to realise the ambitions we'd set. We knew that we'd locked ourselves into the 'death by meeting' trap that Patrick Lencioni unpicks in his book of the same title (published in 2004) and we wanted to escape that before it was too late. Recognising that we all had growth mind-sets, we undertook a series of personal development challenges out of which the realisation came that, yes, meetings were all well and good, but they needed to be short, succinct and with clear, concise outcomes. Furthermore, we now knew they needed to be time-limited and scheduled at a certain time, on a certain day and on a regular basis. It was quite a revelation and it's a practice we've continued to implement ever since, without fail. For example, these days my sales team meet daily at 11:58 precisely. The reason for setting such a specific time is that it sharpens people's minds because it disrupts the norm by which meetings usually occur on the hour or half past. At 11.58, you have to think about it. The result is that nobody is late because it has become an automatic default. Yes, it does take some adjusting to so that it becomes a habit.

Of course, as is to be expected, it wasn't a walk in the park for everyone in our business to adopt this habit and in the early days there were numerous absentees or late entries to meetings, but we persevered because we recognised the significance of this innovation. Today, my brain responds to it on its own body clock – I don't need to think about it. By the time 11.45 comes around, I'm already gearing up for that sales meeting and at 11.51 my heart and mind are in sync with that meeting time, ready for 11.58, knowing that it will finish on time, seventeen minutes later.

Unlike the old days, we now follow a simple structure for these meetings:

- What were our critical numbers yesterday?

- What personal wins did we have?

- What 'stuckpoints' did we have?

- What are we going to do today?

For the sales team, this creates a regular rhythm of knowing the intended outcomes of the meeting and what they will do today, which will then be reviewed tomorrow. They also meet on a weekly basis on Wednesdays for an hour from 2pm. Similarly, our management team check in with each other daily at 10am for ten minutes and every Tuesday at 2.30pm we hold a management tactical meeting for an hour.

The result is that we've been able to reduce the number of meetings while at the same time increasing our time efficiency. The meetings are structured with clear agendas, are direct and very much focused on outcomes. There's no need to waste time on waffle and generalities, and if ever we do need to extend a meeting beyond its set time limit, it needs to be for a very specific and special reason. Every attendee contributes with their updates, or questions, because they all feel invested in the meeting and its outcomes. That's a major reason why it's so important to be able to recruit the right talent to the business, since all input is valuable no matter how small or significant it is on the day. Our rhythm and discipline mirror our mindset, and we marry our hearts with our minds. This allows us all to monitor the health of the business on a daily basis whereby we can listen to its heartbeat and determine if any issues need our attention, or if we simply need to bring some team members up to speed on recent developments. These meetings now play an important role in our continual learning, business growth and revenue growth, and that's the real advantage we, as an SME, have over bigger corporations who often seem to hold meetings for meetings' sake. We're more about driving the business forward during our meetings.

Think about these questions:

- What's your rhythm?

- How strong is your discipline?

- Do you have meetings just for the sake of it?

- Don't you have any meetings?

I'm asking you to think about these questions now in respect of your own business because I often see others roll their eyes at the thought. They think that being their own boss, or an entrepreneur, sets them free from such 'constraints'. I know where they're coming from as I used to share that 'shiny new penny' syndrome. Yet, in all honesty, my business would not have grown to the extent it has today without me finding our own rhythm and discipline. From being unconvinced, I now see that having meetings in my life provides stability and a solid platform to work from. It's not only good for me personally, and the people I work with, it also allows the business to keep its finger on the pulse of what's going on. In essence, we can often manage the business in a small number of short meetings on a Tuesday and Wednesday, with the rest of the time focused on revenue-generating/asset-building activities. That, to me, is an extraordinary outcome in itself, especially armed with the knowledge that all our teams are involved in discussion and diagnosis.

We have gone to great lengths to recruit and reward our talented teams, and in return, through rhythm and discipline, they support the business with clarity. Not only that, these structures allow any problems and opportunities to come to light more quickly, resulting in us being able to turn them around faster. This removes a great deal of pressure from the senior team and prevents them from trying to handle everything themselves (thus freeing them up to work on new initiatives for the business). More importantly, it allows our employees to self-manage, which again allows the senior team to be more hands-off.

Below is a sample agenda that we set which clearly defines the structure and objectives for a meeting.

Agenda – daily sales huddle

Outcomes sought from meeting (succinct, bulleted):

- Introduction
- Critical numbers for yesterday against target
- Stuckpoints

- Goals for today

- How we achieve them

- Close

Letting the car drive itself

As with any business owner wanting to build their concern in order to sell, you need to take your hands off the steering wheel and let the car drive itself. That's impossible to achieve without establishing rhythm and discipline. The ultimate aim for you as the leader is that, in time, you won't need to attend many management meetings at all. Your team, that talent you selected through your recruitment process with due care and attention, will chair meetings themselves, working to the agenda with identifiable outcomes which they will then monitor and review. What you then do with your time is up to you: increased leisure time or working on key revenue areas and long-term business development plans that require time away from the humdrum of daily life.

If you're serious about wanting to scale up your business then you need people to be self-managing in key areas without the whole shebang being incumbent on you. If you can set things up in such a way, it'll happen regardless of whether you're there or not because rhythm and discipline are embedded. I like to look at it this way: say a premiership footballer is about to kick off a match, but not all of the team turn up to play until the referee blows the whistle. That wouldn't be acceptable, and they'd be on the defensive from the get-go. It would never happen, of course. The team would all be on the pitch five or ten minutes prior to kick-off, warming up. Why wouldn't we as businesses not replicate that when it comes to meetings? I have witnessed this in some organisations, where team members arrive late, even if only by a minute or two, and this smacks of a lack of accountability, respect for others and the importance of the meeting. It's simply not acceptable practice in my business; our team members value the rhythm and discipline that is now part of their habitual practice and they'll often arrive five minutes early, ready to warm up. Similarly, they're accountable for achieving the goals minuted and set in those meetings, following the SMART format:

- **S**pecific

- **M**easurable

- **A**chievable

- **R**ealistic

- **T**imebound

Having rhythm and discipline, therefore, helps every one of us to be accountable for our goals and outcomes.

These are fundamental principles to hold if you want to grow your business and be a success and they're completely compatible with embracing your growth mind-set and personal development. I've seen not only our business grow as a result, but many others too.

9
Marketing

Naturally, for any business to thrive, it needs customers. They hold the ultimate power over us in what we pay ourselves and our employees, and whether we remain open for business, or not. It's vital, therefore, that we provide great products, services and experiences in order to attract, retain and develop customers. Of course, this sounds all too obvious, but you'd be surprised at the number of business owners I meet who spend time scratching their heads wondering if the customer really is at the centre of their business, and if so, are they entitled to get what they ask for? In such cases, I have to wonder to myself if people like this really understand anything about marketing at all.

The term 'marketing' covers a huge myriad of approaches with seemingly a similar amount of job functions to support them. No wonder it can be confusing, especially when first considering what's really meant by 'creating a brand with lifetime values'. In my view, it's too easy to muddy our marketing waters, and so, in this chapter, I want to begin by addressing the real basics that underpin marketing and to focus on creating leads and opportunities. These are simply the most important elements that your business needs to turn its attention to first. It's not about creating that super-brand known up and down the country, it's about wanting to get to the next stage in creating opportunities to bolster your sales pipeline that will ultimately lead to more sales. That's what's important to small businesses in the first instance – knowing where the supply chains exist and how the business can fill the gaps. This is especially important if the business is aiming to scale up and create more leads. Relying mainly on referrals is less likely to achieve the outcome you want. Therefore, so that your business can compete with the large corporates, make your mark and open that tap of quality leads which then flow into your business. Size does matter but, in your case, being a small business does actually work in your favour. You need to bring on your 'inner guerrilla'.

As a small business, you have the distinct advantage that you can respond and pivot far more quickly than any of the corporate giants. I know this from our own experience, a relatively small marine business competing against giants. They've got the money, the power and the reach to run rings around us and stamp us into the dirt, if they wanted to. But because they're so vast and encumbered by long chains of command, responding to market conditions is like trying to turn on a floating sixpence an oil tanker going full steam ahead. It's virtually impossible, unless you have six to twelve months to spare. Where we have the edge is that in using 'guerrilla tactics', we can respond to market conditions at full thrust and, like a jet ski in comparison, change direction quickly and disrupt the waters by creating maximum impact. Our very size allows, invites even, adaptability which in turn alters the marketplace at the same time, made all the more possible through the regular, defined and disciplined meetups with our teams that I outlined in the previous chapter. It's why the last item on our weekly sales agenda is always 'marketing intel'. Our team is populated with growth mind-set talent: each regularly listens to podcasts, reads news feeds and researches the market within their specialism. We therefore receive a huge influx of marketing intel into the business. This allows us to pivot almost instantly and to chase new leads. With the onset of social media and online channels through which we can now connect, it's more possible than ever to gain immediate access to this market intel and to monitor campaign data analytics and ROI as they develop in real time.

Understanding which online channel is right for your business is key, whether you are aiming for organic growth via search engines, paid-for campaigns using Google and Facebook, or acting as a result of interactions following a blog or post article on LinkedIn, etc. It will require some investment of both time and money, but the good news is that it needn't be a huge amount. The main point is that you need to remain focused and proactive.

Since I began my business, the marketing emphasis has shifted from the 'push' approach where you encourage customers in through deals and offers to 'buy, buy, buy', to one that now needs to *pull* them in. Customers want more value, and they enjoy reading great content and information so that they can build up trust between them and your brand. Make no mistake, customers will more than likely want to carry out their own online research into your business as well as its products and/or services before they buy from you for the first time. Never before has the presence of your 'social proof' been so important in marketing terms, so it's up to you to provide as much information and content as you can in order to establish any kind of meaningful relationship that will then convert into a sale. Give them information so that they can make the right decision along with the social proof that you're working with the right people. They *want* to consume your guides, ebooks, case studies and testimonials.

LinkedIn

If that's making you pull your hair out because it's another item to add to your to-do list, then don't lose sight of why you need to do it; it's because you want to increase the visibility of your business so that it can grow and scale up. Even if you don't yet have your own marketing department, it'll be worth the effort and minimal expense required to take these steps. For example, we use LinkedIn and find it very effective in reaching out to B2B leads through posting a combination of outsourced and in-house-generated content. This is an excellent way of leveraging your brand. If you provide interesting and insightful content, you'll begin to create a following and establish trust that will eventually create more leads from people viewing re-posted video content, blogs or articles, or even as a result of you commenting on other thought leaders' posts.

I was staggered recently to learn that my own LinkedIn followers are now in excess of 24,000, but that has been the result of constantly creating *valuable* content to the market in all forms, which I've then posted on the platform. Yes, it takes a lot of patience over time, but only ten minutes a day to build that amount and, to be truthful, for a while I wasn't seeing any results from it. Until, that is, I noticed that I was receiving more and more likes, followed by comments starting to creep in. The one thing I didn't do was give up: I kept posting my content. Then, almost as if from nowhere, the tide turned and I was engulfed in a wave of enquiries as people began to engage with me, pulled towards me because they viewed me as a leader in my field of expertise. I can confidently say that at the time of publication I receive at least ten new leads per week via my feed, fifty-two weeks of the year. That converts to at least a five-figure sum in revenue on a monthly basis. As a channel for attracting marketing leads LinkedIn is becoming more and more powerful and can't be ignored. Feel free to take a look at my profile, here:

www.linkedin.com/in/steve-coulson-49b3ba2

Facebook

Like many businesses, we've created our own Facebook page. Although Facebook is a more consumer-facing platform, it still remains the biggest of the social media channels online. It's an ideal place for us to post video footage from which we attract a surprising number of B2B leads. As with LinkedIn, the typical Facebook user is looking for interesting and engaging content, much of which we repurpose from one platform to another. Facebook's mass market reach means that almost anyone who uses the internet will have their own personal page, and that includes potentially new business leads for us too. The main advantage is that we can reach people through their interests and hobbies, and on Facebook that's a much larger audience. Its advertising model is incredibly sophisticated and allows us to target very specific people though identifying job titles and interests, and this represents an amazing opportunity for us to reach those leads. No matter what your business sector is, thinking creatively about your target leads will allow you to segment your own efforts.

In addition to our Facebook page we also created a presence on its platform called 'The Drone Community'. This acts as the top of our funnel for people who want to train as drone pilots. The intention is to build a group as big as we possibly can from which we can then filter those wanting to take part in our courses and lifetime learning. It's another one of our proactive efforts to extend our reach into leads that we can pull towards us, and even though we are a B2B operation, it's surprising how many of the regular consumers we reach then convert into customers looking to purchase a £20,000 drone for their business. We place a huge importance on getting our research just right so that we can aim for powerful targeting. Our ROI is a staggering 20:1 – for every £1 we spend we take £20 in sales.

YouTube

One search engine that's often overlooked by marketers happens to be the second biggest in the world: YouTube.

It's *the* place to showcase your video content. For our business, doing this was one of the best decisions we ever made. In my opinion, it's the ideal channel for a small business to post evergreen material that never dates. For example, some of the most watched videos are of plumbers or DIY merchants showing how to fix a problem with the kitchen sink using their tools. Want to know how to seal a bath? Then there's a YouTube expert to show you, and what's more, you can click on their link and order the parts for overnight delivery. These videos represent high value to the viewer and we've followed their lead by creating useful, informative content on how to best use a drone, instead of one of us droning on (pardon the pun) about how great the industry is. For example, the response to the following video we posted was phenomenal from a lead generation perspective.

COPTRZ TV – DJI Matrice 210 Demonstration (34k views): www.youtube.com/watch?v=0-m-QFsLn5M

- It was an engaging demonstration of a new drone, the video was well timed as it had just been launched and these were the first products to hit the country before any competitors.

- Thermal camera, flight, various camera feeds with examples of optical zoom.

- Engaging presenter and product demo going into detail through spec and features of M210.

- Product comparison from an older existing drone.

- Clear call-to-action at the end of video: Visit website or call our team.

- Actions by customers following video: unknown.

When we compared this video to an earlier one we created, we realised why it hadn't performed as well.

Coptrz CAA Drone Training Testimonial (117 views): www.youtube.com/watch?v=8XQLQAnGCBk

- Highly designed intro going into flat PowerPoint style slides, not consistent.

- Zoomed-in images rather than video content.

- Interview looks as if conducted in a holiday park or someone's living room.

- Position of camera is straight on and looks odd, not very engaging to watch.

- Interviewer continues speaking while the other person is trying to speak.

- Doesn't end with a call-to-action, no description, no tags and no links.

Direct mail lives on!

Who sends direct mail now? We do, but why? The short answer to that is, nobody expects it any more. You'd be surprised, however, just how disruptive this dinosaur can still be. In fact, until recently (in our marine business) we still used the good old fax shot, once the epitome of new communications technology but long considered to be dead in the water. That's great news for us, because so many businesses we target still retain a fax line and a machine. It's perhaps one of the most disruptive means of reaching potential new customers I can think of. Imagine this: a lead you've been trying to reach receives in their inbox dozens, if not hundreds, of prospecting emails per week (that's if they're not already filtered into spam and junk mail) and the likelihood is that yours will be one of the many that is deleted or left unread. A fax, on the other hand, once sent, can often still get printed and ultimately land on the desk of the prospect. For novelty factor alone it's an attention grabber. Obviously, fax machines are effectively dead and long gone in the vast majority of industries since the adoption of email, but it still might be worth your time and effort checking whether your potential leads still maintain a fax (for example, solicitors, shipping companies, etc). In fact, one of our biggest ROIs resulted from a fax shot campaign in 2015 and I believe the fax machine in our old business still hasn't been sent for recycling.

Exhibitions vs demonstration days

In my experience, the time, effort and costs related to attending exhibitions as an exhibitor have never really provided a satisfactory ROI. For a small business looking to scale, it's an expensive option and while your brand might experience the 'halo effect' in creating a lovely glow, it's not a marketing route I recommend. Instead, we moved into trialling a number of demonstration days in which we invite our customer base to visit us, either at our office, or at a hotel facility that we hire out at a fraction of the cost compared to exhibiting. These have been highly effective marketing events during which we control the agenda for our captive audience, and demonstrate our products while we have their 100% attention. What works for us is that we create an event for pre-positive leads which has an exclusive feel about it. The fact people actually turn up means we know they want to engage with us and our products, and that they fully appreciate the lengths we go to in order to look after them on the day (including tempting and tasty refreshments).

Events such as demonstration days are ideal for a business looking to directly engage with its customers, existing and new. Such events allow the business to express its brand with authenticity, in real time and with real feedback from the people who matter most in the equation – the customers. The next task is to convert those leads into actual sales.

10
Sales

During the course of my mentoring, I've met some highly intelligent people who run their own businesses, but I'm often amazed at just how many seem to have no sales expertise or processes in place, or understand the basic psychology of selling. They then wonder why they're not able to sell their products or services. When I question them as to who's responsible for their sales division and what experience they have, they usually reply along the lines of, 'I've employed Bob to do that' or 'We take it in turns'. This tells me straight away that they're lacking some very basic understanding of what skills are required, but it still often leaves me flabbergasted.

In this chapter I'll explain the process I use to create, inspire and activate a team in order to convert leads into sales. Knowing as you now do that I place huge importance on developing your own growth mind-set, this is the point at which all the dots connect that will help your business grow and scale up.

As I've previously explained, your values are the foundations on which you can successfully build your business. The talent you've recruited should all be aligned to these values so that everyone, across all divisions, is aiming for the same outcome. Your salespeople in particular have shown they have an abundance of 'intelligence, energy and attitude' (the IEA bundle) and if you've followed my recruitment process (Chapter 7) you already know they're aligned to your foundations and values because:

1. They're intelligent, as you've already determined, and are able to assimilate their knowledge of your products/services (especially if highly technical) which they can use to inform and educate leads.

2. They're full of energy, since without it, they'll not acquire new customers.

3. They each have a 'can-do' attitude and a growth mind-set. They are proactive, intuitive and can solve problems on the fly. They crack on with the job, overcome hurdles no matter what, and are masters of their own destiny.

This is a good list of the personal characteristics a great salesperson should possess. If Bob is more likely to take a ninety-minute lunch break, is slapdash about the office with an untidy desk and never stays a couple of minutes beyond 5pm, then perhaps he's not the one who'll go the whole way for the business. And I don't blame him for that, if nobody has ever explained to him the vision, mission and values that underpin the business. Or, perhaps you've hired that seasoned sales professional with years of experience, who sounds and looks slick on paper, but is probably simply biding their time until they can take early retirement. I mean no disrespect to these people. I have to say, however, that in my experience, the graduate intake we employ meet all of our IEA criteria. They are all prepared to go that extra mile, not simply because they're hungry for success themselves, but also because they've invested in the values and beliefs of the business. Plus, they know that the more successful they are in sales, the more people in the business will participate in its success.

Interestingly, many of our own sales personnel are young, former sports professionals, so not only do they care about their physical well-being, their mind-set is attuned to pushing themselves to the limit. They possess a state of mind which is intrinsically linked to maintaining their energy levels, an important asset to a salesperson. Good degrees of intelligence are also vital so they can relate to, and understand, the product or service which they can then convey to the customer with authority. The people we employ in sales tend to fall into the top

30% of the population, based on their intelligence test results. We value them highly and we pride ourselves that they work with us. We actively want intelligent people who aren't afraid to challenge the status quo – because they're naturally and positively disruptive.

That doesn't happen overnight. Once we've identified the right people with their IEA potential, our work with them begins in earnest. We nurture and train them thoroughly because, at the end of the day, we don't want to end up with a team made up of Bobs who disappear at 5pm each night without a backward glance at the business they're working in.

Sales masterminding

Our nurturing process is central to our sales team training. Unlike many businesses that hold a sales meeting on a monthly basis, we schedule meetings weekly. In my opinion, monthly meetings aren't nearly as effective because whatever is discussed and agreed is easily forgotten four weeks later. The major-ity of our weekly sales meeting sessions are devoted to role play and this is a key training tool that underpins our products and services; it's an activity that keeps us *all* aligned to our core principles. It's not simply an opportunity for us to have a kick about and have fun (although we do have a lot of fun) and nor do the team roll their eyes and think it's all just a waste of time playing pretend. Our sales mastermind sessions, as we call them, are rooted firmly in the experience of the business of selling to our customers. It's a safe environment in which team members can voice their concerns or address issues they're facing, such as not being able to convert a lead into a sale. It's the ideal scenario to role-play problems, and to find solutions as a result of interplay, devil's advocacy and collaborative thinking. We rarely leave a role-playing session behind without a solution that our sales team can then employ with real customers. So many business leaders underestimate the value role play offers as part of their sales training process, or they don't believe it will deliver measurable outcomes. I disagree, and profoundly so, when the alternative I see all too often is a bog standard, tick-box exercise and answering multiple choice questions.

Our salespeople love to rise to the challenge role play presents and, for us, it's a positive investment in our future sales growth. Our energy meets their energy, head on, our desire to disrupt fuels their disruptive capabilities, our passion for learning feeds their need to learn, our values are theirs, and theirs are a reflection of all that we stand for as a business. Jointly, we discover new things about ourselves, our business, our processes and our customers, and we do that weekly, which I believe reinforces our collective will to excel. If more businesses would only adopt this as part of their sales process, I'd guarantee they'd see more opportunities to grow, to move forward and, ultimately, sell more products, faster.

It's simple: rehearse, rehearse, rehearse. Our business relies on being able to demo our products and services, and so our salespeople must be prepped well enough to demonstrate 100% familiarity, expertise and authority without a moment's hesitation. The last thing a customer wants to see is a salesperson fumbling around with a piece of kit, or trying to get the product to work properly if it all goes south at the most inappropriate moment. I've always admired presenters on live TV shopping channels who've been handed a whiz-bang food blender only moments before they go on air, but nothing goes to plan. No whiz, no bang. They're not even sure how to turn it on, and in all likelihood it's not a food blender at all but a fancy solar-powered paint stripper. My point is, sales teams need to know their product inside out, to the very last detail, so that when they're asked a technical question by the customer, they can answer immediately and with authority. Their fluency will allow them to explain all the features and benefits, but also the value it represents to the customer. That's why we rehearse, rehearse, rehearse so that the demos can run without a hitch. They're allowed to get it wrong in the training room, where it's safe to do so. In front of a customer, the demo has to be spot on. The more you demo, the more you sell.

For example, some of the products we demo have an 80% conversion rate.

The five-step sales process

I'm passionate about sales and getting it right. There's a reason why I've left sales to the latter part of this book: my belief is that, if you don't connect all the dots in your business, beginning with you, then your business won't grow. Once you start to see how all the dots fit together by aligning your vision, mission, values and strategy to your processes, you throw your business the lifeline you've been looking for, and you will start to see growth. Where there's no sales process, however, there's no means of tracking, converting and measuring results.

Our five-step sales process is one we've developed over the years, which includes our BUY IT NOW model that will guide any business through the essential elements that will convert prospects into more sales:

- Prospecting (going in cold)
- Qualifying
- Objection handling / pitching

- Negotiating

- Closing techniques

Prospecting (going in cold)

We're the first to acknowledge that all prospecting can be tough, but that's why we place so much emphasis on the IEA attributes when we recruit our salespeople.

If your sales derive from B2B, don't even think about prospecting if you're not willing to embrace a growth mind-set mentality, because cold calling (as it used to be known) isn't for the faint hearted. Whether your team is using the phone, direct mail, knocking on doors or, more likely these days, selling via social media platforms, you need to know which is the most effective method and the one likely to convert from a lead-in activity. We've created KPIs for each activity we use most frequently that carry a valuation in terms of effectiveness of the activity as follows:

- Phone call – 1

- Video post – 10

- Webinar – 25

- Meetings and virtual meetings – 25

In this way, we can track our leading indicators and prospecting activity. For example, our sales team also use Soapbox (see Chapter 7) to reach leads when they've not been able to make direct contact via the phone. They create and send a short, snappy personalised message to the lead along the lines of, 'Trying to get hold of you. Would like to talk to you about these three things and I can save you this much.' Using Soapbox is a highly effective tool as it allows split-screen technology so that the salesperson can remain in view while posting up a visual. They then email the visual to the lead in the knowledge that video content is the consumed media. For the social media savvy sales graduate, this is second nature selling. Our salespeople will also front a Soapbox video for evergreen content that they post on our social media pages (LinkedIn/Facebook), which will include their direct contact details for follow up. We encourage them to be prolific in their output and, in many cases, certain salespeople become synonymous with a particular product (a fast-growing trend in prospecting).

Qualifying

If you don't qualify a marketing-generated lead or prospect, you run the risk of wasting precious time and money chasing something that's not real. There are numerous qualifying resources available online, each with their own specifications, but in principle we qualify all our leads using our own BUY IT NOW methodology:

Budget

- Does the potential customer have a budget?
- If so, does it have to go to tender?

User's story

- Is there a known history that might persuade the purchaser?

Yes or no person?

- Who decides?
  - The lead you're currently talking to?
  - An individual budget-holder?
  - A committee?

Intent

- Is the purchase a necessary one or a 'nice to have' for the client?

Tinker?

- Is the lead tinkering with the market and looking at your competitors? If so, what differentiates you from them? Adjust your sales pitch accordingly.

Needs

- What are the most important benefits to the customer in terms of product specifications and purchasing options?

Outlook

- When will the customer decide?
- When does the customer want to take delivery?

What next?

- Is this a one-off purchase?
- Discover if there are further opportunities for the order to be multiplied if the customer is part of a wider organisation.

Where possible, engage leads in conversations to discover what their priorities, needs and demands are. The more you can learn, the more you can qualify the lead as a potential customer that will convert into a sale. It might seem laborious, but it works. The fact is that you'll save time in the long run with all the knowledge gained from qualifying, and you'll know how to pitch better. As a result, your conversion rates will improve. You will also be able to measure and track progress with a greater deal of certainty.

Objection handling/pitching

Most salespeople struggle at this point because they don't know how to handle an objection. They don't realise that, in fact, an objection is also a signal for buying, which explains why 99% of salespeople capitulate after five objections. Once a salesperson can identify what those objections are, they will use them as weapons to strengthen their hand, and if necessary, deal with them for as long as it takes. In such a case, your salespeople will be elevated into the top 1% of sellers because they'll go beyond those five objections and get to close the sale. How is that possible? By understanding the principle of 'feel, felt and found'. For example:

> **Customer:** Your price is too expensive.
>
> **Salesperson:** Thanks for that. I understand how you *feel*. Other customers have *felt* the same when they first looked at the pricing. What they've *found* is that when they actually look at what the return on investment is over [a period of time] they're actually getting 100:1 return on their investment. So, the expense is insignificant compared to the returns you're going to get with our solution.

The top salespeople will also find it useful to isolate any objection with 'Is that your only objection?' If the customer continues with more objections, then each can be dealt with individually until, eventually, none remain. Ultimately, your potential customers will respond more positively when they're handled with empathy, sensitivity and understanding. An aggressive salesperson is likely to end up arguing with the customer (**never do this!**). Such an approach is highly likely to result in a no-sale and no future order enquiries from the prospect. A sales process and methodology eliminates this risk and instead facilitates closing the sale. That's why I emphasise the need for recruiting, nurturing and training the right salespeople, and why rehearse, rehearse, rehearse through role play is a crucial tool.

Negotiating

Having successfully fielded any potential objections, it's likely the customer is interested in moving towards a purchase, but often they want to negotiate a better deal before they sign a contract/part with money. This is the point at which the inexperienced salesperson can fail in their attempts to close the deal. While the topic of how to negotiate well in order to win *good* business could fill an entire book, the outline below shows the key skills we expect any good salesperson to possess (bearing in mind they've already been through a thorough recruitment process and participate in weekly meetings in which role play and rehearsal have a huge impact on their outcomes). Without the correct level of IEA, this is when I often see many SME sales divisions making a series of common mistakes and failing to close a successful deal. The last thing any of us want to do is leave hard 'cash on the table' to win over the customer, yet I'm often staggered by how many salespeople believe this is the right way to go. As a very last resort, maybe, but when you start taking cash out of sales as standard practice, the business will inevitably falter. From the outset, you need a negotiating strategy that your salespeople under-stand and stick to.

The first and lazy port of call for salespeople will be to knock off a percentage of the price (a discount), even for first-time buyers. Anyone with any degree of buying savvy will go for a cheeky 10% off any price. It's the salesperson's job to show the prospect that they're paying for value and to counter the dis-counting disease as means of securing custom. Any business owner who believes that it's a good idea to discount on that basis needs to reverse that picture and think in terms of the actual hard cash they're giving away. For example, if your product or service is priced at £10,000, then a 10% discount is £1,000 in your customer's pocket, not yours. However, the customer can still be satisfied when the *perceived* discount amounts to 10% but when the direct cost to the business is minimal. For example, offering the equivalent of £1,000 in maintenance/support or training that would normally command far bigger margins, but in real terms costs significantly less to provide. It's a big value win to the customer and minimal cost to you if training is £200 to provide in actuality. To operate in this way, salespeople must be prepared in advance, both with their offer and how they deliver it, which is when the meticulous rehearsal and regular role-play sessions come into their own. They need to be able to act with authority and on their intuition in order to leave as little, or no, cash on the table. I'm happy to credit this technique to the book *Give and Take* by Chester L. Karrass in which he advocates that if you do need to give anything away, always ensure you can loop back to value. If you do have to give something, make sure it has a high perceived value to them and low cost to you.

Closing techniques

One of the biggest problems with salespeople is they don't do this last step and they'll do anything to avoid the rejection that comes with a 'no'. The most basic part of this should be: so what happens next towards confirming an order? Very often, business owners tell me with frustration that it progresses only as far as what I call 'the cup of coffee' meeting which invariably results in salespeople saying 'they're getting back to me'. That's usually because the salesperson has a fear of rejection, or lacks the right mind-set, training and the necessary IEA to close.

Assuming they've gone through the pre-qualifying process, there's no reason not to ask the customer plainly, 'Can we have your order?' At the very least, any inconclusive effort needs to be followed up with a firm plan of action, such as contacting the customer again the next day and heading off any attached fear of rejection. Even then, if the response is a most definite 'no', it's far better knowing now than three or more meetings later, when it's plainly obvious there's no business to be had. However, if handled correctly through a rigorous sales process, it will all link together. Therefore, if the salesperson doesn't qualify correctly, they'll face more objections further down the line. If they don't handle objections well enough, they'll find it hard to close because the conversation has looped back again to those objections and they won't need to negotiate, let alone close.

That is the beauty of having a sales process: it might seem to involve a lot of up-front time and energy on your part to get to this stage when all you want to do is sell, sell, sell. However, while there is no such thing as a 100% conversion rate, you'll want to get it into pretty high figures so that your business can grow, so why wouldn't anyone want to give it their best shot? It certainly won't happen by chance or by charm alone. Your salespeople must be ready, primed and have the right balance of IEA to achieve results and get anywhere near step five of my process, again and again.

Leads united

Based on the five stages that we've already covered in the chapter, what you need to do is to make sense of this so that you can see how all the elements I've described link together. View the process as if it were a funnel, with two different taps that you can turn to adjust the flow accordingly.

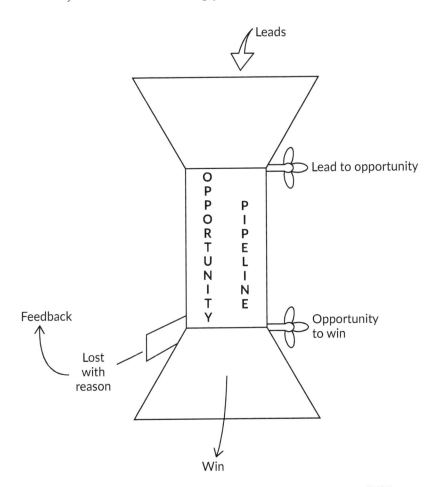

At the top of your funnel, as shown in the diagram, are your leads, wherever they come from. They may be from your own prospecting from marketing or they may be from referrals. However, as they stand, they're just leads and nobody can be 100% certain which way they'll go. Only by qualifying will the salesperson know if the prospective sale has the potential to sink or swim. With a swimmer, it becomes an opportunity to which a value and timescale can be assigned. Our standard is to aim for 20% or more of all leads to become opportunities based on the following judgements:

- What is the quality of the leads you've sourced?

- What percentage of your leads can convert to opportunities by tweaking your offering?

Obviously, not all leads will convert into immediate opportunities for a variety of reasons, but those that you have qualified as having real potential can be placed in the 'opportunity pipeline' where each has a value. For example, at any one time, you might have ten companies where each represents an opportunity of £50,000 and so you now have a £500,000 pipeline. The next big conversion rate is in translating that from an opportunity to a 'won' conversion rate. Again, this is a percentage (our standard target conversion rate is 50%) and it depends on how good your salespeople are at objection handling, negotiating and closing. Any positive result that emerges from the funnel with a confirmed order is the 'won' rate. For example, with our 50% conversion rate, we'd expect, for every ten opportunities, five will be 'won' and five will be lost/ deferred to a later date. Using your own funnel it's possible, therefore, to view what's happening, and where, within the process.

In the top segment, there's a tap which represents the lead to opportunity conversion rate. Below that sits the opportunity pipeline with another tap which filters down into your opportunity to win conversion rate. In monitoring the flow of leads into the opportunity pipeline, you can determine where bottlenecks are slowing down the process that feeds into the 'won' segment and where you need to turn the taps on full. It's a constant process of evaluation and manipulation. Over time, you can turn the taps to increase the conversion rates within the funnel that can create a paradigm shift in your business fortunes. Knowing which areas in the pipeline – prospecting, qualifying, objection handling, negotiating, closing – need attention is key to understanding the numbers critical to the business' growth forecasts, and in knowing the velocity at which the pipeline is functioning. There's not much to celebrate and get excited about if a £10m pipeline is going to take ten years to convert. That's the beauty of the qualifying stage.

Knitting it all together

Everything I've described above is all well and good providing you follow a process along similar lines. However, unless you utilise a CRM (customer relationship management) system, believe me, things will soon begin to get a bit messy. In fact, I think CRM is a misnomer because, for me, it's a *sales enhancement tool*. I know that some business leaders go pale about the gills when I mention this, a bit like they did when I talked about embracing vision, mission and values, but once they understand there is a real need for it, then the colour returns to their cheeks. Their major fear is that it sounds expensive and needs all sorts of fancy software and data input. Which of course it can, at the high end, if you have the resources (and need) for it, in which case, go for it. But free online resources, such as Trello, are just as good, or it can be as simple as creating your own spreadsheet, as long as it's maintained and updated daily. I'm so often staggered at how many business-people don't actually know what their salespeople are up to because they have no process and central-ised, standard cross-company system. They literally prepare and send quotes from their own computers without any reference to each other, or even the busi-ness owners themselves.

Any form of standardisation and centralised CRM tool you can implement, which can be viewed and analysed in real time, offers an instant snapshot of where the business is right now and, perhaps more crucially, where it's heading and how fast it's grow-ing. Being able to look at it and talk about it in your weekly sales meetings with the best talent you've recruited along the lines I suggest above, you'll be confident knowing that you have employed good, sharp salespeople who will manage the funnel effectively and productively without wasting valuable time and effort in chasing dud leads. This integrated process must stem from the business leader's own growth mind-set as this connects all the dots that ultimately lead to sales growth. Because if they're not selling more every month, every quarter, every year, they're not going to grow. One aspect of my mentoring business owners that I enjoy is seeing the pennies drop in their minds after I've helped them realise why their business is failing to grow, mainly due to a massive hole in their sales process which they've never really understood, or applied with any meaningful practice. Without a proper sales process that can convert, measure and track actual sales, there is no business. Having a process in place literally can reverse a business' flagging fortunes.

CASE STUDY: DANNY

When entrepreneur Danny came to me for advice, he was selling automation system components into the offshore oil and gas industry. Leading from the front, he'd sold these systems globally into an industry he had already worked in as an employee for other companies for ten years, so his knowledge and experience was second to none. Deciding to go it alone, he had set up his own business and had seen some strong growth over his first two years. By the third year, however, the company had slumped from a £2m turnover down to £1.7m and now it was getting bogged down with incorrect orders, late shipments and disaffected customers.

To counter the decline, Danny recruited two additional salespeople in an attempt to reorganise and regenerate the fortunes of the business. After six months, the new salespeople were still struggling to make any real difference to the bottom line and Danny was on the verge of firing them.

Seeking my advice and insight into his business, we lifted the bonnet on the sales department and immediately discovered the problem. Danny had always been a lone-wolf salesman in his previous employment and had brought the same ethos into his own business. The main problem we identified was that all his systems were ones that he carried in his head and there was no such thing as a defined process in place. So the business lacked any clarity in respect of quoting systems, there was no CRM in place and no pipeline visibility at all! Little wonder that the new sales recruits stood no chance of success, or of measuring their performance. The first thing we put in place was an inexpensive cloud-based CRM system that still managed to deliver huge value to the business through sales visibility and formalisation. As a result, Danny was able to advise and coach his small sales team around their pipelines and he could also identify problem areas by having a daily dashboard of:

- Activity
- Conversion rate of leads to opportunities
- Conversion rate of opportunities to won deals
- Pipeline values
- Sales booked

As a result of implementing a methodical sales process, in the fourth year Danny saw a his turnover increase to £2.5m and by the fifth year this further increased to a whopping £4.1m and 20% net profit (EBIT), despite very challenging trading conditions in the oil and gas sector at the time.

11
Money

Like it or not, there is a residual fear, even among people in business, in talking about money. Many are even too worried to look at their personal bank accounts for fear of what they might see, and I can relate to that well, having been there myself until I recalibrated my relationship with money via my business. If we could all only break through that taboo and be more familiar with the concept of talking about money more openly. Especially if it's bad news, because that's the time when you need to make decisions and manage things going forward, such as cashflow (which can bring anyone out in a cold sweat from time to time). Avoiding talking about it is possibly the worst tactic any business owner can adopt, especially during more difficult times. It only adds to stress, people start to close down and make poor decisions, and the people around them notice how irritable they've become. Morale drops, performance slows and the business grinds to a halt. If we could all only embrace our growth mind-sets and learn more about the true value of money, and how central it is to the life of the business, day in day out, minute by minute, second by second, then the lifeblood of our business would flow more freely and keep the heart alive.

Money isn't simply the end-game reward of your enterprise; it's connected to the whole business. While that might seem obvious (and who doesn't keep an eye on the money in their business?), it's surprising how little attention it gets outside of revenue generation and paying the bills. I realised early on that money wasn't my strong point, until I began to recalibrate my understanding of it, and now my view of it has changed completely. In this chapter I'll be sharing some facts that I either had to learn the hard way, or as a result of revaluing the value of money.

Management accounts

Thinking back to Chapter 8 when I described the rhythm of a business and its heartbeat, now imagine that money is the blood of the business that runs throughout its veins. Otherwise, it's dead. That's why you have to have a velocity of money running through the business, and with positive pressure to make everything work, as well as enough spare to act as working capital. If your business was a patient in a hospital (because, in all honesty, the reason you're reading this book may be because it's possibly not functioning in the way you want it to) then the doctor would first check the vital signs and, from them, form an understanding of how healthy the body was. It's the same with money: you need an understanding of money's vital signs and how these affect the business. The patient record in this case will be your management accounts. Otherwise, you've no way of knowing how well you're doing, or if you're looking a little poorly, which makes a prognosis difficult.

The big learning for me was getting to grips more with the management accounts. It's not exciting in all honesty, it's the really dry, but essential arse-end of the business that gives you the fuller picture of how well the business is doing. Coming to terms with these accounts is certainly not something you should avoid doing, and I recommend your accounts are drawn up (ideally) on a monthly basis or, at the very least, quarterly. If you don't employ your own in-house finance person with the competency to prepare them, then engage an accountant to do this for you. It's not expensive, and by seeking recommendations from your local business peers, you'll soon source a reputable accountant they trust. It's essential, there's no excuse for putting it off if you want your business to grow and scale up. All it requires is someone to prepare your:

- Profit and loss account

- Balance sheet

- Year-on-year comparisons

As soon as possible, allow your growth mind-set to enable you to learn what you don't already know about money and accounting. There's no lack of printed material and courses dedicated to financial management for non-financial managers and I'm adamant that investing in this learning was one of my best areas of business growth. I wish I'd understood more about money when I first started my business instead of passing the buck to a bookkeeper and hoping for the best. At least these days, even though I'm no financial wizard myself, I can ask the right questions, interpret results with more confidence and respond more quickly when money becomes an issue. Having a growth mind-set and wanting to learn as much as I need to, I've reached a point where I can query and question an accountant and ask, 'What does this mean?' That question serves you well, especially when you ask it on a regular basis. It's ludicrous to ask this once every twelve months only to discover that while you might have sold twice as much as the previous year, your overheads have spiralled out of control, and/or your unit cost price isn't anywhere near what you thought it was. In fact, you've probably been selling at a loss. The truth is, a year down the line might just be too late to discover your shortfalls, when the business is on its knees and you can't turn the situation around.

Success and profit

Money needs to flow with velocity around the body of your business. If your ambition is to grow your business beyond its current position, then how can you know what success is if you don't actually determine whether it's growing in a profitable way? Even if your strategy might not be to generate short-term profits, you still want to grow and increase your market share – and for that, you not only need money, you need to *understand* it. That's why, by knowing your numbers inside out and being familiar with them on a regular basis, you'll identify how well the business is performing and, if needed, pivot, adjust, shift, cut back, throw more in, or whatever you need to do in order to keep the business vital. It's not enough to rely on your gut feeling alone and hope that it's right, because I can tell you from my own experience (which is typical) that gut feelings aren't anywhere near as reliable as knowing the hard facts.

I love the fact that I am constantly empowered through learning and I've certainly made my recently acquired knowledge of money work for me. Save the butterflies in the belly for the inspiration and dream part of the journey and let your head, not your heart, do the talking when it comes to money. Knowing that I can see and understand how the business is faring, and that the business body is healthy, allows me to sleep at night. When you get to really know money, you immediately see the areas where you can save money, because you understand better how it affects your profit and loss in your balance sheet. If you're building your business to eventually sell, you certainly need to have an understanding of this. When I began this book by talking about having a growth mind-set, I wasn't encouraging you to sit cross-legged on a beanbag sipping on a chai tea; I wanted you to begin making the links between a growth mind-set and *all* the elements I've covered in this book. A growth mind-set equals me being able to help my business grow, and to ultimately make more money. Not just for me, but for the really talented people that I work with who will benefit from the phantom share scheme. They all know what the business is worth, they all possess similar growth mind-sets and all have an abundance of IEA. We're all driving for a common goal and striving to outwork the competition, because we all know what's at stake. If you've never considered a monthly management meeting about money to be the most exciting day at the office, then perhaps you should think again. It's only numbers, adding up and taking away, but keeping on top of them is priceless in terms of business.

When I explain my relationship to money in this way to the SME business owners I mentor, I can literally see the colour rushing back to their cheeks, having gone pale when I originally asked them about their management accounts process. From that point forward, they begin to value money in a completely different way. What's your relationship to money been like so far?

Remember:

- Understand the basics.

- Take a course, it needn't cost you much, and take advantage of as much mentoring as you can.

- Management accounts – run them monthly in order to have a clear view of how well the business is performing.

- Cashflow forecasts – have them prepared for you on *at least* a monthly basis. If, and when, you become a highly scaling business, you need to know what's going out as well as still having to fund that growth, and know that you can. Know what the demands on your cash are.

- Accountants – seek recommendations from your peers or people you trust. It'll be a small investment, but in terms of understanding your monetary health, it's essential.

12
Learn, and Learn Some More

When you joined me on this journey, you were either about to embark on setting up your own enterprise, or you were feeling stuck in a rut with your SME business and had lost sight of your ambitions to grow and scale up. Having made it to this chapter, I hope you feel better equipped, and now have a clear framework to be able to make this happen. Remember, in the beginning, it all started with you.

I hope this book has been revealing and rewarding, and has enabled you to reconnect with your original dreams and aspirations which, if nothing else, has served to remind you that, hopefully, you began your own journey from a position of having a growth mind-set. I've been at pains to show you that I recognise how it feels when the going gets tough, as clarity fades under the daily pressures of keeping heads above water. It's all too easy to forget the reasons that originally drove you to set up in business in the first place, or to step up to that promotion into a leadership role. The insights, tools and advice I've shown you should now encourage you to believe once more that you *do* have the potential to achieve more and to grow and scale up your business. That's why I've prompted you to face some of the barriers head on, with brutal honesty, and to accept that where there are gaps in your knowledge, you need to make time for learning to overcome them. Assuming you're ready to learn more, this is a sign that your growth mind-set remains alive and healthy. Remember: working on your own self-development is an investment you can't afford to ignore. The more you can grow as a business leader, the more your business will grow in spades as a direct result. Having refreshed your perspective on yourself in relation to the business, you can examine the key areas where the processes I've described connect in a flow that stems from embracing your growth mind-set. That includes identifying and articulating your vision, mission and values, through to creating processes and rhythms to facilitate recruitment, sales and marketing while always understanding the importance of money as a key indicator of future business growth. These are the lifeblood of your business which keep its heart pumping.

I guarantee that once you start to learn, you'll be pulled towards learning more – not just about your business, but about yourself. Your imagination will be fired up as you spot new opportunities that ensure your business disrupts and stands out from the crowd. What were seen as barriers to growth are now challenges that you'll face with increased confidence, relishing the chance to experiment and take more risks, allowing yourself to fail fast. That isn't the same as failure, it's the product of a growth mind-set abundance rather than scarcity. The more opportunities you spot, the more you'll work and the luckier you'll be. That's the sum of my experience and the pathway to success I wanted to share. Like you, I know I couldn't have done this on my own. I truly value the mentors and meetup groups that have supported me and opened my eyes to learning. Some were already ahead of me in the game and they'd trodden the same path I was on. It's so much easier to navigate your way through the jungle when the person ahead of you has cleared a path. Through them, I realised my own potential and where I needed to grow if I wanted my business to do the same.

Mentors don't choose you – so be proactive in your search and you'll find the ones that are right for you. For example, if you're intending to scale up in the technology sector, it makes sense to select a mentor with a similar experience of scaling up in that industry. The magic of joining a mentoring mastermind group, in which a variety of business sectors are represented, is that you'll also learn lessons from other leaders whose experience will be valuable for your own. From my perspective, I gain as much satisfaction from helping entrepreneurs through the processes I've described in this book as I do when I witness their own businesses transform as a result.

CASE STUDY: JAN

Jan runs a web-based and wholesale concern selling novelty gifts and homeware. When she asked me for advice, she was undoubtedly very talented in sourcing products from the Far East and then shipping them to the UK market. Jan had great products, but she was literally doing everything in the business. As a result, its annual turnover was stagnating at £300k per year, and worst of all, Jan was paying her employees before herself. That didn't stop her from working all hours and ensuring her small band of employees were looked after, but she was totally involved in all aspects of running the business. If it was growth she was hoping for, it wasn't happening, and her business was stuck. The first thing we did together was to deconstruct what her business actually was and identify what tasks she was doing. We also made sure that she took a wage straight away because, in actual fact, the business could/would find a way to bear it. Although Jan had great processes when it came to sourcing and developing products, she had none in place whatsoever in respect of marketing and sales, or for any other back-end part of the business. Taking on board the same advice I've described throughout this book, we set up a series of processes and fired those people who were, frankly, taking the mickey and only turning up for their pay packet. Jan's problem was that she was fiercely loyal and very ethically minded towards her employees, but by the same token there were one too many who knew that and took advantage of her. Until, that is, she changed and asked herself some brutally honest questions. She took time to reconnect with her woefully underused growth mind-set and started to learn more about business from other people's experiences.

She worked on identifying the vision, mission and values of the business and for the first time created a strategy. Jan also learned how to attract and recruit the talent that could best serve the business and, as a result, she saw marketing and sales performances improving and a significant increase in turnover. Appreciating the role of money now played a critical role in Jan's understanding of the business and within three years it grew from being stuck at £300k per year to £3m and a seven-figure valuation, ready to sell and making her able to consider embarking on a new business opportunity. It might come as no surprise to discover that Jan is now a mastermind mentor.

Outcomes such as this are one of the biggest reasons that get me out of bed in the morning. If I hadn't taken the plunge and embraced my own growth mind-set, sought insights from others and engaged with my own learning opportunities, I might never have been in the position to grow and scale up my own businesses and I might just still be all at sea.

13

Conclusion

When I started writing this book, I wanted it to be just that bit different from the numerous self-help titles that explain in great detail how to do this, or how to achieve that, in business. Don't get me wrong, I think they're highly valuable assets for any business leader to engage with, especially in terms of theory and implementation. I've read many of them myself and they've each provoked thought, discussion and action, as well as feeding my growth mind-set with their insights.

Learning, as you now know, is a central part of my own personal and business development and there's no doubt in my mind that we all need to spend more time learning. What I've discovered, however, is that there are few business books that adopt a belt and braces, down-to-earth approach grounded in the everyday experiences that I've been through myself. Through my own mentoring of other SME business owners, I identified a gap in such peer-to-peer knowledge-sharing. Many simply want some good old-fashioned advice so that they can either start, or reset, their business and allow it to grow. Their growth mind-set might currently be akin to an oven set at gas mark 1 (at least that indicates they've switched their growth mind-set on and are ready to go it alone). They want to ratchet up to gas mark 10, but they're scared of turning up the heat too quickly. They've made a start but don't know what to do next because they may have hit a glass ceiling and, as a result, they're not able to see the way forward towards growth. What they lack is a real person to act as their mentor, a helpful guide with experience, knowledge and wisdom, to see them through those early stages of the business with ambitions to scale up.

That's why I wanted this book to be experiential, as opposed to theoretical – at the end of the day, although over a period of time I've established a number of successful businesses, I'm still a 'normal' person (with the normal hang-ups and loads of flaws). I wasn't creating unicorn enterprises promising to change the world, but I did want to change *my* world for those nearest and dearest to it. I'm no different to the chap you'll see in your local pub one night supping on a pint (there's good chance it could be me, if it's followed by several more), or going to the match at the weekend. I'm no Richard Branson or Jeff Bezos, although all credit to them for what they've achieved. However, when I was starting out, such iconic role models could have alienated me from my own dreams and aspirations because I could never compare with the billionaires, so why bother in the first place? That's a great achievement for them but not everybody will be a billionaire. Of course, I'm not suggesting you can't become a billionaire after reading this book, but I think for most of us, if we're really honest, what we'd like most is to be successful, fulfilled and happy. Oh yes, and being a multi-millionaire will do nicely too!

I'm certain that you'd like to earn more money, have a better lifestyle and, probably, you'd love to be a lot less stressed. That's why I hope this book will help you on the first steps of that journey. The vast majority of the book has been drawn from my own direct and personal experience. I wanted to reflect my business narrative arc in a way that could relate to any SME business leader who wants to emerge from their current doldrums, wishing they could reconnect with their dream and see their enterprise ultimately grow and scale up. I had the same aspirations when I began my first business, and after a period of struggling and not seeing the results I was aiming for, I knew I couldn't do it on my own. I needed to seek out mentors who'd trodden a similar path and who had overcome obstacles. I yearned to discover what was good – no, *great* – practice over standard practice, to correct common mistakes I was making in my business without realising I'd made them. I wanted to know my purpose – what got me out of bed in the morning and how I could pass on that passion and enthusiasm to the people that worked for me. Learning from others, reading books, listening to podcasts and talks was the key to that. Until then, I'd never really made the link between the value of learning and implementing those lessons in my business. I quickly began to love learning with an eagerness that never ceases as time passes. It soon dawned on me that learning was, and still is, absolutely core and organic to business growth and development. Not only did I learn so much about myself and my values, but the business also started to grow as result. I began to build a business populated with people who were completely in alignment with me, the business and its values, vision and mission, and because I'd sorted out the problem of recruiting the right people, they understood and executed its strategies with perfect precision. Learning turbocharged my business growth and focused it with absolute clarity on being ultimately able to serve its customers.

In the face of growing globalisation, trade wars and uncertainty, starting or growing an SME can seem like a daunting activity, and understandably so. That's no reason to give up on your hopes and dreams for creating a better life for yourself, your family and the communities in which you operate. Obstacles will always present themselves and they can either block your path or present opportunities. But you can learn how to avoid and circumvent them. When you find yourself stuck and not knowing which way to turn, there's always someone who will help you. They might have written a book, produced a podcast or be a mentor as part of a group. One thing you can be certain of is that they have walked in the same shoes as yours. When my business faced down one of the biggest economic crises in recent history, we didn't do that alone. Having a growth mind-set and the willingness to learn helped navigate the difficulties, and learning from others and expanding our horizons brought new perspectives in being able to scale up the business in ways previously unimaginable.

SMEs, like yours, are the economic backbone of the nation and it's in all our interests to help each other thrive through sharing our knowledge and experience. Whatever you experience, learn along the way, cherish it, nurture it and, most of all, embrace the journey with an open heart and arms, and a growth mind-set. Who knows, someone, someday, just might ask you for help, and that will be an achievement in itself worth celebrating.

Learning Resources

The following list is presented as a useful kick-start to your learning. It is by no means an authoritative list, nor does it represent the sum of everything I've read or engaged with over the years. I hope you will be inspired to read these titles and more, and to embark on a continuous lifelong learning journey of your own.

Books

Blount, Jeb, *Fanatical Prospecting: The Ultimate Guide to Opening Sales Conversations and Filling the Pipeline by Leveraging Social Selling, Telephone, Email, Text, and Cold Calling*, Wiley (2015).

Collins, Jim, *Good to Great*, Random House (October 2001).

Collins, Jim and Porras, Jerry, *Built to Last – Successful Habits of Visionary Companies*, Random House (September 2005).

Gerber, Michael E., *The E-Myth Revisited: Why Most Small Businesses Don't Work and What to Do About It*, Harper Business, 3rd revised edn (March 2001).

Karrass, Chester L., *Give and Take*, Harperbusiness, revised edn (1995).

Lencioni, Patrick, *Death by Meeting: A Leadership Fable About Solving the Most Painful Problem in Business*, Wiley (March 2004).

Moore, Rob, *Life Leverage: How to Get More Done in Less Time, Outsource Everything & Create Your Ideal Mobile Lifestyle*, John Murray Learning (2016).

Peters, Steven E., *The Chimp Paradox: The Mind Management Programme to Help You Achieve Success, Confidence and Happiness*, Ebury Digital (2012).

Sharma, Robin, *The 5am Club*, Harper Thorsons (December 2018).

Sinek, Simon, *Start With Why: How Great Leaders Inspire Everyone to Take Action*, Penguin (2011).

Other resources

IADD Podcasts

Marketing School

The Productivity Show

Entrepreneurs on Fire

The Disruptive Entrepreneur

The Salesman Podcast

Masters of Scale

The Author

 A successful businessman, Steve co-founded and scaled a maritime systems business from conception through to its sale, for an eight-figure sum, to a large PLC. Concurrently, Steve co-founded and is currently the MD of a scale-up commercial drones enterprise that is forecast to hit revenues of £20m+ within the next two years.

Additionally, Steve worked in the family wholesale-to-retail fashion business, which he grew and sold, and he currently co-owns a property business with his wife.

Steve's business success so far has attracted various awards including two Queens Awards for Enterprise and a place in the FASTTRACK 100.